ESSAYS ON WAR AND PEACE: BIBLE AND EARLY CHURCH

Willard M. Swartley, Editor

Occasional Papers No. 9

Institute of Mennonite Studies
3003 Benham Avenue
Elkhart, Indiana 46517

1986

POLICY STATEMENT FOR THE <u>OCCASIONAL PAPERS</u>

<u>Occasional Papers</u> is a publication of the Institute of Mennonite Studies and authorized by the Council of Mennonite Seminaries. The four sponsoring seminaries are Eastern Mennonite Seminary (Harrisonburg, VA), Goshen Biblical Seminary and Mennonite Biblical Seminary (Elkhart, IN), and the Mennonite Brethren Biblical Seminary (Fresno, CA). The Institute of Mennonite Studies is the research agency of the Associated Mennonite Biblical Seminaries.

<u>Occasional Papers</u> is released several times yearly without any prescribed calendar schedule. The purpose of the <u>Papers</u> is to make various types of essays available to foster dialogue in biblical, theological and practical ministry areas and to invite critical counsel from within the Mennonite theological community. While most essays will be in finished form, some may also be in a more germinal stage—released especially for purposes of testing and receiving critical feedback. In accepting papers for publication, priority will be given to authors from the CMS institutions, the College Bible faculties in the Council of Mennonite Colleges, the Associate membership of the Institute of Mennonite Studies, and students and degree alumni of the four seminaries.

Because of the limited circulation of the <u>Occasional Papers</u>, authors are free to use their material in other scholarly settings, either for oral presentation at scholarly meetings or for publication in journals with broader circulation and more official publication policies.

Orders for <u>Occasional Papers</u> should be sent to the Institute of Mennonite Studies, 3003 Benham Avenue, Elkhart, IN 46517.

Editor: Willard M. Swartley, Director
         Institute of Mennonite Studies
Associate Editor:
         Elizabeth G. Yoder, Assistant Director
         Institute of Mennonite Studies

ISBN 0-936273-09-7

Printed in USA

CONTENTS

PREFACE

This issue of <u>Occasional Papers</u> contains two contributions to each of the three literature groups encompassed in the title: Old Testament, New Testament and Early Church (after the first century). Millard Lind's book analysis supplements the second contribution.

The first two essays, addressed primarily to interpretation of issues in the Old Testament, focus on the use of violence from two quite different but not uncomplementary perspectives. The first essay locates the meaning and significance of **herem** in relation to the holiness of God which calls for **herem** not only in warfare but in other aspects of life as well. On the basis of this study one might contend that **herem** is not inherently a violent practice, but only circumstantially so. The second essay argues that human violence gives rise to and is held in check through sacrificial ritual, the means of atoning for human violence. If violence in warfare is considered phenomenologically, the contributions of these essays raise for further study the interrelationship between the divine and human bases for violence, not to mention the subsequent--but usually priorly discussed--question of divine and human agency. We must also put into conversation with these theses the significance of the biblical claim that God's nature is also **hesed**-love. We must then seek to understand how this relates to both **herem**-- rooted in divine holiness--and atonement, especially in the culminating disclosure of God-in-Christ, on the cross.

The two New Testament essays, Dyck's and Lugibihl's, again put in tandem relationship two emphases which stand partially in tension with each other, but nonetheless belong to the same gospel and are in the final analysis not uncomplementary. Stuhlmacher's bold thesis that Jesus as messianic Reconciler provides a hermeneutical key for the unity of the New Testament must be evaluated not only on the basis of the emphases he cites but also on the basis of the portrait of Jesus presented by Lugibihl's article. Along this axis of discussion much liberation theology would fault Stuhlmacher's thesis as too one-sided in its understanding of the work of the Messiah. The peace of the Messiah has a revolutionary ferment upon the social, political and economic structures that Stuhlmacher's emphases do not include. Nevertheless, his contribution of this emphasis to New Testament studies deserves our careful and grateful response.

The two articles on the early church of the second
to fourth centuries come at a time when a spate of new
publications on the topic have mined the evidence anew
to support the opposing traditional interpretations of
the sources (e.g., Hornus' pacifist interpretation
versus Helgeland's et al. and Swift's recent works).
In my judgment, Elster's most original article
contributes significantly new perspectives for the
debate. His amply documented thesis is far-reaching
in its implications. If indeed "the new law of
Christ" phrase regularly referred to Isaiah 2:4- and
Matthew 5:44-type of understandings, then the
consequence of this upon the rationale for the
virtually universal nonparticipation of Christians in
the army prior to AD 170 merits consideration by
scholars in all traditions. Friesen's article
provides a helpful complementary contribution in that
it shows both the diversity of practices and factors
and the constancy of certain emphases in the
development within the early church on this matter.

This issue of Occasional Papers is different from
preceding ones in that it brings together essays
written initially by seminary students as research
papers. Most were written for the course, War and
Peace in the Bible, taught at the Associated Mennonite
Biblical Seminaries by Millard C. Lind and Willard M.
Swartley. John Friesen's paper had its beginning in
course work at Canadian Mennonite Bible College. To
be sure, each of the contributions has been revised
extensively; editor Swartley did further revision on
both the Pries and Dyck contributions beyond the
normal editing function.

In the context of seminary education many papers
similar to these are produced, finding their way into
seminary professors' files or student boxes in
libraries. As editor of this series I welcome comment
on the priority that Occasional Papers should give
to make such material available in this form. It is
my sense that this collection makes a distinctive and
very useful contribution to the ongoing discussion of
war and peace issues. Your evaluative response as
reader and user will be appreciated.

                                    Willard M. Swartley, Editor
                                    September, 1986

HEREM IN THE OLD TESTAMENT: A CRITICAL READING

Mark Fretz

Herem[1] is used in each of the three sections of the Hebrew Bible (Torah, Nebi'im, Kethubim). With its extensive usage and connection with the question of war, one might assume that it has been fully researched within biblical scholarship. This is not the case. It is dealt with, but usually as a sub-topic. A study focusing on the quest to understand the meaning and usage of **herem** is requisite.

The usage of **herem** in the Old Testament can be investigated in a number of ways. Our discussion of the material follows the order of the Hebrew Bible. We examine the Torah (Pentateuch) first. This portion of biblical material is important because it confronts us with three major elements of our discussion: the law material, the traditions behind the text, and the category of "Holy War." The second portion of the paper deals with the Nebi'im (Prophets). The "Early Prophets" (Joshua through 2 Kings excluding Ruth) provides a narrative history of Israel. Both the Deuteronomic history and the Israelite conquest are treated here. The "Later Prophets," (Isaiah through Malachi excluding Daniel) treat the prophetic criticism of Israel, the people and the institutions. The Kethubim (Writings), the last section of the Hebrew Bible, will then be analyzed. The final major section of the paper is an attempt to move beyond the Old Testament material to see how **herem** may have been used in later history and what implications result from the transformation of usage observed throughout the study.

Two points must be set forth initially. The reading of the Bible is the basis of this study. The primary material is best understood when it speaks for itself. To this end we attempt to take the text literally, or "read the text straight."[2] Such an attempt assumes that the reader is aware of his/her assumptions and can keep those assumptions from "coloring" the reading of the text too greatly. The assumption made here is that a word study is really a concept study. Therefore, not only the use of **herem** (syntactically, grammatically, contextually, literarily, etc.), but also the terms used in relation to it (as synonyms or antonyms) are critical for a proper understanding of the term. It is assumed that

the Bible is a collection of literature written over a
long time span. This means that the use of a term may
change with the changing times. Second, the
Anabaptist concern about war and peace is an impetus
for this study. The commitment to Yahweh as God and
to Jesus as the Messiah is reason for desiring to
understand the apparent dichotomy between the Old
Testament God of war and the New Testament Prince of
Peace. We proceed from this basis.

I. **Herem** in the Torah

The Torah covers the first five books of the Bible.
We shall deal with it in two parts: first, Genesis
through Numbers, then Deuteronomy. This not only
divides the number of occurrences of **herem** evenly
but also is an attempt to recognize the "Source
Theory" in biblical scholarship. Noting how and where
the term is used within the Torah may shed light on
the meaning as the writers understood it. A
discussion about types of law (the law codes; types of
law--casuistic, apodictic, or participial; preaching
the law; proverbial law, etc.) would greatly enhance
our comprehension of **herem** as it is used in the
Torah.[3] We turn to this prior to considering the
usage of **herem** in the Torah.

Although law as we have it in the Old Testament is
a corpus of written material, it was developed in oral
form through daily experience in ancient Israel. One
type of law, casuistic law, defines a situation and
states the legal consequences, "When . . . then" or
"If . . . then." It deals with general cases usually
considered "secular law" (Exod 21:1-11[4];
21:18-22:16; Lev 12-26; Deut--many sections). This
type of law is the standard Near Eastern law type.
Apodictic law, on the other hand, is
characteristically Israelite. It is divinely given
law that takes the imperative form of "Thou shalt" or
"Thou shalt not" (Exod 20:3-17,23,25,26; 22:20-33; Lev
19; Deut 15:1; 16:19; 16:21-17:1; 23:2-8). Motive
clauses which give incentive for obeying the law occur
with apodictic law.[5] In addition to these dependent
clauses there are longer hortatory compositions known
as parenesis. Parenetic material is advice,
preaching, or exhortation that is found in the midst
of law material. This type of material occurs more
frequently in later texts than in early law material.

Participial law is a third type of law in the Torah. It usually begins with a participle and ends with the legal consequence (Exod 21:12-17;[6] 22:17-19; Lev 20:2,9-13,15,16,27; 24:16). It may be translated, "The one doing 'X' shall receive punishment 'Y'." The participial laws of the Old Testament are few and occur within other law material.[7] Death (**Mot-yumat**) is the consequence for each case we observed in the Old Testament.

TORAH REFERENCE CHART. See Appendix I, pp. 29-32 for usage details (V-Verb; N-Noun; Literary forms: Law types - A-Apodictic; C-Casuistic; Pt-Participial; LI-Legal Instruction; PL-Preaching the Law; NA-Narrative; Numbers with a, b, c represent word meanings given on p. 30-32).

Ref.	Use	Lit Form	Ref.	Use	Lit Form	Ref.	Use	Lit Form
Genesis -	None		Lv 27.29	V 5a	LI/C	Dt 3.6(b)	V 1a	NA
			27.29	N 2	LI/C	7.2	V 2/5a	A/PL
Ex 22.19	V 5a	Pt	Nu 18.14	N 1c	PL	7.2	V 2/5a	A/PL
			21.2	V 3	NA	7.26(a)	N 1b	A/PL
Lv 27.21	N 1c	LI/C	21.3	V 1a	NA	7.26(b)	N 1b	A/PL
27.28	V 5b	LI/C				13.16	V 5a	A
27.28(a)	N 1c	LI/C	Dt 2.34	V 1a	NA	13.18	N 1a	A
27.28(b)	N 1c	LI/C	3.6(a)	V 1a	NA	20.17(a)	V 5a	A
						20.17(b)	V 5a	A

Herem is noticeably absent from Genesis. This eliminates its use in the pre-Abrahamic epics and sagas as well as the patriarchal stories. Exodus, Leviticus, and one of three references in Numbers set **herem** within the context of law code or ordinances. These occurrences are somewhat peculiar. Exodus 22:19[8] is part of a group of three verses of participial law set at the end of a section of casuistic laws ("when, if") and just preceding a section of apodictic laws ("thou shalt"). Leviticus 27:21,28,29 are part of a chapter of ordinances which deal with devoting or vowing within the cultic setting. The type of material in vv 21,28,29 is "Legal Instruction" regarding cultic regulations. It has a casuistic (when, if) structure, but does not appear to be casuistic law strictly speaking. This whole chapter seems to be appended to the extended "Holiness Code" which ends with the blessings and curses of Leviticus 26.

Numbers 18:14 is part of a section of material (Num 18:8-32) which is considered "traditional P." **Herem** falls within a narrative where ordinances are being "preached" in a fashion similar to what one might find in a modern day instruction manual regarding religious behavior. The topic and type of material (Preaching the Law) is similar to that found in Leviticus 27, but it sounds more directive (apodictic?), "All **herem** in Israel shall be for you."

In Exodus, Leviticus, and Numbers the type of material seems to be discontinuous with that which is around it. **Herem** is used both positively and negatively (Lev 27). It is sacrifice to Yahweh both as banning or setting something apart strictly for God, and destruction of something or someone vowed to be destroyed utterly. Each of the references is found in a cultic setting.

Numbers 21:2,3 is a unique case in the Torah of Israel making a vow of **herem** to Yahweh before a battle. Extra attention is paid to these verses because they closely relate to Gerhard von Rad's concept of "holy war." This "sacred vow" to destroy the enemy, made in the cultic milieu, is central to holy war as von Rad understands Israel's warfare. These verses are a separate story inserted into an "E" narrative section chronicling the wanderings of Israel in the wilderness. The **herem** vow takes the form of covenant-making with God which is conditional ("if...then"). This is preparation for war (v 2) and Yahweh is the agent of **herem** (v 3, according to the Hebrew text and contrary to the RSV rendering "they"). It must be noted that this is the only instance of Israel explicitly making such a vow prior to war that we observed in the biblical materials. Elsewhere Joshua or other individuals make statements implying that the Israelites have made this type of vow before going into war.

When reading the Torah we must be aware of the various "traditions" that may exist within the text. These traditional sources are not hard and fast fact, but rather are part of a hypothesis that attempts to deal responsibly with the history of the text. Observing which sources, in what context, and its content is useful in our quest to understand how **herem** is used.

Exodus 22:19 is part of the "Book of the Covenant" (Exod 20:18-23.33), which is considered to be independent of any source.[9] **Herem** is used to mean "utter destruction" of a person for sacrificing to a god other than Yahweh. This is the only occurrence of **herem** as part of the participial type of law, although the consequence of participial law in the

Bible is always death (cf. p. 9). Note that this
independent (early?) source connects **herem** with
sacrifice.

Leviticus 27:21,28,29 and Numbers 18:14 (cf. above,
p. 9, 10) are part of the "traditional P" source.
These constitute seven out of the ten occurrences of
herem in Exodus through Numbers. Source P deals
with matters of the religious cult, and these verses
fit that theme well. The ordinances in these verses
are difficult to categorize. We consider Numbers
18:14 among the parenesis material that weaves the
narrative with the preaching of the law. **Herem** in
this source is used in a fairly consistent fashion
(Num 18:14 is an exception) and relates to the single
theme of cultic devotion or banning. **Herem** is used
to mean devoting or banning something or someone to
God, either being holy and set apart from regular use,
or being profane and dedicated to be destroyed
utterly. Note the prohibition against redeeming in
Leviticus 27:28,29. Numbers 21:2,3 is part of a
narrative section of the L or N[10] tradition (see
above p. 10).

We can conclude from our observations about **herem**
in the various sources that sacrifice and cultic
devoting or banning predominate usage. **Herem** is
used most extensively by P and the L or N tradition
uses it in a way unique to the Torah, as a vow in
preparation for war.

In Deuteronomy, the last book of the Torah and the
first of the corpus known as "Deuteronomic History"
(Deuteronomy through 2 Kings), **herem** must be seen as
it appears in the Torah portion along with its use in
the Nebi'im portion (the Early Prophets) of this
history. Two points stand out in Deuteronomy's use of
herem: the emphasis on holiness and the importance
of **herem** in Israel's wars. We pick these up as they
arise in the biblical text.

Herem occurs eleven times in three sections of
Deuteronomy. The first introduction (chaps. 1-4) uses
herem in historical war narratives (Deut 2:34; 3:6).
This utter destruction of the enemies' cities and all
inhabitants raises the topic of "holy war." Israel's
use of **herem** in war is a key element for defining a
war as holy war, according to von Rad.[11] Most
scholars accept this as a category, though some offer
alternatives, but inevitably **herem** is discussed as a
sub-topic of holy war. The use of **herem** is viewed
as a device utilized to re-create the sacral ordering
of the holy war.[12] Von Rad states that, "The most
important thing for us is that the obligation to put

under the ban was conceived by the Jahweh faith as an act of acknowledgment of Jahweh and his help."[13] The problem of treating **herem** as a category of holy war is two-fold: (1) **Herem** in Israel's wars does not make such wars "holy" (semantics/theology) and (2) when **Herem** is understood only as a holy war concept, its use outside that context is not given a fair reading (exegesis).

The holy war category is rejected and challenged by some scholars. Smend argues that the place of **herem** in Israel's wars finds historical ground in the covenant of the early confederation. This covenant demands obedience to Yahweh and **herem** is a part of "Yahweh war."[14] Weippert examines the component parts of holy war as von Rad views it and finds historic parallels to them in the ancient Near East.[15] The conclusion is that holy war as recorded in the Old Testament is not a late reinterpretation of war narratives that differed much from the early interpretation of the war event. Theologically there is the tendency to view **herem** as part of a holy war and equate **herem** in war as something holy. Craige emphatically states that such extermination cannot be regarded as holy.[16] Israel's use of **herem** in war made them religious, but not holy. Taking this position also assists us in avoiding the mistake of equating Israel's enemies with Yahweh's enemies. Holy war as a category is questionable, and studying **herem** under this category may distort our understanding of the term as part of Israel's war and nonwar usage. **Herem** occurs as part of some of Israel's wars, yes, but its meaning in other contexts must not be predetermined by assuming its meaning as part of holy war.

Herem appears four times (Deut 7:2[2x]; 7:26[2x]) in the second introduction (chapters 5-11). These chapters are Moses' exhortation to Israel, including the decalogue and other laws. A preaching of the law regarding wars is the literary form of chapter seven. Deuteronomy 7:2,26 both have an apodictic sound to them, "Thou shalt not...", as well as motive clauses (7:4-_ki_; 7:26-"or you will be fit for destruction just like it"[17]). This is the first _rule_ connecting **herem** to war.

The motive here is holiness. Israel is to avoid becoming contaminated. To this end, in war the enemy is to be destroyed utterly. Holiness in this setting means purity on the sacral-cultic, social and economic levels. Israel sacrifices the conquered city and people to Yahweh. This is religious. The extermination of the foreign populace helps them avoid intermarriage (social) which has its effects in the cultic realm (Deut 7:3, 4). Economically there is a ban of things related to the foreign cult that are made of silver and gold (vv 24-26). This prevents both the worship of idols and the accumulation of booty by individuals committed to the foregoing covenant (Lv 5-6).

The Deuteronomic Code (Deut 12-26; 28) contains four references to **herem**. The sanctuary is the initial topic of this law code, followed by warnings against idolatry (ch. 13). A city that has turned to idol worship is to be treated like the cities of foreigners in the conquest (Deut 2:36; 3:6; 7:2,26). Deuteronomy 13:16 and 13:18 are apodictic law types set within parenetic material. There is emphatic command to destroy the entire city, people, animals, and objects or metals; the **herem** is for that off limits. This is the paradigm for viewing **herem** as utter destruction that can be visited upon Israel (Josh 6-8; Isa 43:28; Jer 25:9; etc. regarding the destruction of Israel and Judah).

Deuteronomy 20:17 uses **herem** in the context of laws to be observed in war (cf. Deut 7). This verse appears to be part of an apodictic law accompanied by a motive clause.[18] The motive is holiness. This verse connects the use of **herem** in law codes to the practice of war. "The laws of war in Deuteronomy 20 are expressed in language reminiscent of the ideology of war contained in the Song of the Sea [sic. Exod 15:1-18], but they are at the same time thoroughly pragmatic from a <u>theoretical</u> point of view."[19] A concept of war without human kingship is assumed. **Herem** is utter destruction of foreign people, animals, cities, and objects in war. It is a war with Yahweh as king, and hinges on Israel's covenant commitment to Yahweh.

In sum, the Torah's use of **herem** is eclectic. Various sources (B, N or L, P, D), diverse literary forms (law types, narratives, legal instruction, preaching the law), and a wide range of usages are evident. There is strong association with the cultic, (i.e. sacrifice, idols, devoting as offering, the priest's portion, banning in war as sacrifice) and emphasis on holiness. Remnants of an early concept of devotion to God are found in the war and non-war references. **Herem** first appears in the history of Israel with the Covenant Code and during the wilderness wanderings. It increases in frequency dramatically in the last book of the Torah (source D).

II. **Herem** in the Nebi'im (Prophets)

Nebi'im REFERENCE CHART - See Appendix I (cf. pp. 30 f for usage details)
(V-Verb; N-noun; Literary forms - NA-Narrative; LI-Legal Instruction; PPr-Prophetic Prose; PPo-Prophetic Poetry; O-Oracle)

Ref.	Use	Lit Form	Ref.	Use	Lit Form	Ref.	Use	Lit Form
Jos 2.10	V 1a	NA	Jos 10.40	V 1a	NA	2Ki 19.11	V 1a	NA
6.17	N 1a	NA	11.11	V 1a	NA			
6.18	V 2	NA	11.12	V 1a	NA	Is 11.15	V 6	PPo
6.18(a)	N 1a/1b	NA	11.20	V 1a	NA	34.2	V 4	PPo
6.18(b)	N 1a/1b	NA	11.21	V 1a	NA	34.5	N 3	PPo
6.18(c)	N 2	NA	22.20	N 1a/1b	NA	37.11	V 1a	NA
6.21	V 1a	NA				43.28	N 2	PPo
7.1(a)	N 1a	NA	Jud 1.17	V 1a	NA			
7.1(b)	N 1a	NA	21.11	V 1a	NA	Jer 25.9	V 4	O
7.11	N 1a	O				50.21	V 2/4	O
7.12(a)	N 2	O	1Sa 15.3	V 2	O	50.26	V 2/4	O
7.12(b)	N 1a	O	15.8	V 1a	NA	51.3	V 2/4	O
7.13(a)	N 1a/1b	O	15.9(a)	V 1a	NA			
7.13(b)	N 1a	O	15.9(b)	V 1b	NA	Ezk 44.29	N 1c	LI
7.15	N 1a/1b	O	15.15	V 1a	NA			
8.26	V 1a	NA	15.18	V 2	NA	Mic 4.13	V 4	PPo
10.1	V 1a	NA	15.20	V 1a	NA			
10.28	V 1a	NA	15.21	N 1a	NA	Zec 14.11	N 3	PPr
10.35	V 1a	NA						
10.37	V 1a	NA	1Ki 9.21	V 1b	NA	Mal 3.24	N 3	O
10.39	V 1a	NA	20.42	N 2	O			

The "Early" and "Later" portions of the Nebi'im are here reviewed separately, but in sequence. The usage of **herem** in the Nebi'im introduces a long continuum of time, a variety of perspectives (Deuteronomist and Prophets), and carries us into a period of developing institutions; the rise and decline of Israel (and later Judah), and the contemporaneity of oral and textual forms for the traditions. Two "critical" issues that emerge in the early prophets are considered: (1) the conquest and (2) Deuteronomic History.

Joshua contains forty occurrences of **herem**, 50% of the Nebi'im total. The majority of occurrences (78%) are part of narrative material; seven are considered part of oracle material. The conquest narrative begins with the Jericho story. **Herem** appears fifteen times in this story (Josh 2-7) with references in chapters 2, 6, and 7. The absence of **herem** in Joshua 3-5 is explained by the

intersplicing of the crossing of the Jordon narrative
in these chapters, between the initial spy mission and
the engagement of battle (chaps. 2 and 6).[20]

The story of the conquest connects Joshua with
Israel's history of religious wars during the
wilderness period (cf. above, pp. 10f.). **Herem** is
understood as an integral part of the battles of
conquest. The utter destruction of the "Canaanites"
is perceived throughout Joshua as the literal
extermination of these inhabitants of Palestine (Josh
6:21; 8:26; 10:28-43; 11:10-23). Some scholars
understand this **herem** as a later theological
interpretation of Israel's history, a rationalization
of the ban.[21] Other scholars agree with this
bias,[22] but understand **herem**, as it was practiced,
differently. It is viewed as a tool in the
socio-economic program of Israel that ensures
community equality and provision in the central
institution, as a means of assistance for the
needy.[23] Accordingly, **herem** is to be understood
as selective control of how booty is distributed, not
wholesale extermination of the populace. Along the
same line, conquest has been pictured as less of a
military offensive from a foreign people, and more of
a "peasant's revolt against the network of
interlocking Canaanite city states."[24] This means
that there was no mass genocide as is suggested by the
Bible's use of **herem**. There was only selective
elimination of royal administrators (of necessity).

What is the truth behind the text regarding the
meaning of **herem**, especially as it relates to the
conquest? There is too much inconclusive evidence on
the issue to make a definitive statement about the
conquest. The theory about a later reinterpretation
of the history has some validity, yet it is inadequate
to respond to the historical reality of **herem** in the
ancient Near East.[25] The socio-economic conception
of **herem** has some merit because it reinforces
covenant equality and acknowledges pre-kingship social
structure. It reckons with the inconsistent
application of **herem** with regard to booty in
conquest battles.[26] The explanation that **herem** is
a means of economic reform must be limited in its
application; there is a much wider use of the term in
the text.[27] The peasant revolt model for the
conquest has archaeological support;[28] it is a
tenable position. My reservation, however is that the
biblical text consistently treats the Canaanites as
the enemy, not a group of possible "converts." The

conquest is understood herein as Israel's process of taking control of Palestine. **Herem** within this context is killing in battle, but the extent of such utter destruction is still open to debate.

A quick observation of the references throughout Joshua reveals that **herem** means utter destruction or the command to destroy in a war context. The Jericho narrative has many connections to the Torah.[29] The repeated accounts of victory over enemies are like the same story with different names supplied. **Herem** is used in all these stories as utter destruction of all living beings (**kal-hanepes**). The final occurrence of **herem** (Jos 22.20) recalls the Achan story (Josh 7) and the law about an Israelite city becoming unclean (Deut 13:16-18).

The structure of the book of Joshua gives clues to the work of a person compiling a larger history. This deuteronomic history continues through 2 Kings. The history contains sections of material that do not fit with the flow of the text.[30] The key point here is the relative unanimity in this material's use of **herem**. The Deuteronomic material contains 51 of the 80 total occurrences of **herem** in the Old Testament (63.75%). The use of the term in this material is predominantly consistent in its war context and meaning of "utterly destroying" the enemy, with some divergence due to the compiled nature of the massive amount of material. To understand the meaning of **herem** in the Old Testament we must both pay close attention to this unit of material and limit the impact of the usage herein on the general understanding of the term. This school of thought represents only one perspective (the Deuteronomistic perspective).

The narrative material in Judges through 2 Kings reflects some comparison and contrast in its use of **herem** as compared to the Torah. In Judges 1:17 the story and the use of **herem** are very similar to Numbers 21:1-3. Judges 21:11 seems to be a test case of covenant faithfulness in Israel (cf. Deut 13:12-18). As in Judges 1:17 there is some modification of application from what is prescribed in the Torah (i.e. selective **herem**: all males, but only females who are not virgins). It must be noted that **herem** occurs only in the first and last chapters of Judges.[31] 1 Samuel 15 contains all eight occurrences of **herem** in the large corpus of 1 & 2 Samuel. It is a transition chapter in Israel's history.[32] Yahweh initiates the action in the form

of an oracle (1 Sam 15:3) based on the exodus
experience (Exod 17:8-16; Num 24:20; Deut 25:17-19).
The law defining Israel's behavior (Deut 20:16-18) is
being tested out in the new context of a monarchy in
Israel. **Herem** in this chapter means utter
destruction of all that Amelek has, according to
Yahweh, but is redefined by Saul and the people to
mean selective destruction of what is despised (1 Sam
15:9; cf. Judg 21).

1 Kings and 2 Kings use **herem** twice in narrative
and one time in the oracle genre. 1 Kings 9:21
recognizes that Israel did not destroy all the
inhabitants of Canaan. These people are made a forced
levy of slaves instead of being destroyed utterly.[33]
1 Kings 20:42 picks up the tone and genre of 1 Samuel
15:3 regarding treatment of a foreign king who is
devoted to destruction.

2 Kings 19:11 reflects the use of **herem** by other
ancient Near Eastern nations. Here Sennacherib, king
of Assyria, in a rhetorical question claims to have
done **herem** to all lands. Mesha, ninth century
B.C.E. king of Moab uses the same root consonants
(חרם) in his stele:

> I fought against the town and took it and
> slew all the people of the town as satiation
> (intoxicating) for Chemosh [the god] and Moab
> . . . I fought against it from the break of
> dawn until noon, taking it and slaying all,
> seven thousand men, boys, women, girls, and
> maid-servants, for I had devoted them to
> destruction (sic. **herem**) for (the gods)
> Ashtar-Chemosh."[34]

A parallel term, **asakku**, is found in the Mari
documents (cf. Appendix II, p. 33), "He of (my)
servants who steals the booty of a soldier has eaten
my asakku (i.e. has committed a sacrilege against
me)."[35] In this instance handling of booty is what
relates to **herem**. Just as in Israel's wars in
Joshua the booty was restricted in various ways from
use, so at Mari the king makes a law restricting the
use of booty. Violation of this law makes the person
guilty of **asakku** (cf. Josh 7). There is some
question about the connection between the Mari
material and biblical use of **herem**.[36] The Moabite
stone is an authentic parallel to biblical use of
herem.[37] The conclusion drawn is that Israel is
not exclusive in using this term. In the ancient Near

East **herem** is applicable in both the religious and the political-military realms.

The later prophets use **herem** thirteen times in a total of six books. There is a diversity of literary material in which **herem** is used (cf. Nebi'im chart above, p. 14). In the major prophets (Isaiah, Jeremiah, Ezekiel) we find ten occurrences of **herem**; the minor prophets contain the other three. Two main issues arise in the major prophets: (1) The "Day of the Lord" and **herem** and (2) prophetic criticism of Israel's people and institutions. The minor prophets pick up the "day of the Lord" theme and push the two-sided nature of **herem**.

Each of the major prophets uses **herem** in a consistent genre. Isaiah uses prophetic poetry, with the exception of Isa 37:11 which is shared with 2 Kings 19:11 and 2 Chr 32:14 in narrative form (possibly borrowed material). Isaiah 11:15; 34:2, 5; 37:11 all are part of the pre-exilic material in Isaiah.[38]

Isaiah 11:15 introduces several interesting aspects of the use of **herem** in the later prophets. It is set in the context of "day of the Lord" pronouncements (11:10,11; 12:1,4) that speak of Israel's hope. This "day of the Lord" saying is discussed by von Rad, who concludes that the images originated in the holy war tradition.[39] These connections between **herem** and the "day of the Lord" must be tempered by the longer and broader tradition of which **herem** is a part. They must also recognize the distinctly different ideas included in the "day of the Lord" references. Isaiah 11:15 is a case in point where **herem** means "to divide" rather than "to destroy utterly" and does not serve as the end of "holy war" at all.[40] Thus, the "day of the Lord" has a broad usage which includes **herem** but it is not to be wholly defined by von Rad's "holy war" category. The imagery of the "day" is both positive (a day when Yahweh will make things right again) and negative (a day when Yahweh will judge and punish) as is **herem** (cf. pp. 20f). The "day" takes on eschatological meaning in some biblical texts, using **herem** to mean "utter destruction" in that context (Jer 50; Mic 4; Zech 14:11 [no **herem**]; Mal 3:19-24).

Isaiah 34:2 and 5 both use **herem** to mean "utterly destroy" as in slaughter. **Herem** also is closely related to sacrifice imagery (Isa 34:6,7).[41] Isaiah 37:11 is in a narrative section which uses **herem** to mean "utter destruction" (identical to 2 Kgs 19:11; 2

Chr 32:14). These "First Isaiah" occurrences of
herem are considered "southern" and early in origin
(ca. 742-688 B.C.E.). The diversity of usage reflects
the flexibility of the term and the writer's mastery
of a term that was in current parlance.

   Isaiah 43:28 is the only occurrence of **herem** in
"Deutero-Isaiah." **Herem** is set within lawsuit
imagery (Isa 43:26) here as is the case in other
classical prophets (cf. footnote 38). The "Servant
Song" context is unique for **herem**. **Herem** is part
of God's recounting of Israel's sinfulness set between
two poems of salvation related to the omnipotence of
Yahweh the "Redeemer" (Isa 43:14-21; 44:1-8). The
judgment of utter destruction (**herem**) is contrasted
with the salvation made possible by Yahweh the
redeemer (**go'el**).

   Jeremiah uses **herem** four times, consistently
within oracles. Jeremiah 25:9 prophesies **herem**
against all Palestine, including Judah; God's
instrument is Nebuchadnezzar.[42] Jeremiah 50:21,26
and 51:3 reverse the roles: Israel is God's agent in
doing **herem** and Babylon is the object. With promise
of God's pardon (cf. Is 43:28), the "day of the Lord"
is present in Jeremiah 50:20 as a day of hope for
Israel. Ezekiel 44:29, placed within legal
instructions regarding the temple, is given a
visionary context (Ezek 44:1-8); yet the ordinances
parallel Torah ordinances (Lev 27: Num 18) very
closely.[43]

   The minor prophets use **herem** three times. The
earliest of these occurrences is found in Micah 4:13.
The theme of the "day of the Lord" is picked up by
this contemporary of Isaiah (Mic 4:1, 6). Several
ideas connect this occurrence of **herem** with Isaiah
and raise an important aspect of prophetic writing.
The "day of the Lord" refers to Yahweh establishing
the house of the Lord. **Herem** means to "destroy
utterly," as devotion to God, reminiscent of Isaiah 34
(cf. Jer 50:21-26; 51:1-5). Micah 5:2 re-emphasizes
the messianic prophecy found in Isaiah 11. There is
diversity of meaning, rather than a single-minded idea
here.

   This diversity in the prophetic material enables us
to see the scope of how **herem** is used in the Old
Testament. In relation to the "day of the Lord,"
herem has nuances of both judgment and hope. The
prophetic dialectic combines and consists of the
visionary and the realistic stances. Isaiah and Micah
show the tension between the cosmic (visionary) and

the principle of promise and fulfillment (realistic) with their use of the "day of the Lord."[44] The perspective of these prophets allows the reader to observe how the history of Israel was not perceived by everyone in the same way. **Herem** is, thereby, freed from one-dimensional usage and meaning in the biblical material. It has the positive hope of holiness as well as the negative destruction of the profane in judgment. It is very real in the past (cf. Num 21:1-3; Josh 6-11; Judg 1:17; 21:11; 1 Sam 15), the present (cf. 2 Kgs 19:11; Isa 37:11; 43:28; 2 Ch 32:14), and also visionary in the prophecy of **herem** to come, (Isa 11:15; 34:2, 5; Mic 4:13; Jer 50:21,26; 51:3; Zech 14:11; Mal 3:24). The "day of the Lord" theme is "redeemed" from artificial synthesis and late theological reinterpretation by the prophetic criticism of the various interpretations of Israel's history. In this process the meaning of **herem** retains its manifold nature and flexibility.

Zechariah 14:11 uses **herem** to mean utter destruction as part of war. This prophetic prose section is considered later material than chapters 1-8 (ca. 520 B.C.E.). It utilizes the historic images of Israel's beginnings, the plagues of Egypt (Zech 14:12) in the context of the "day of the Lord" theme (Zech 14:1,4,6,8,9,13,20,21). The <u>absence</u> of **herem** is the hope and sign of how Jerusalem will "dwell securely." Malachi 3:24 refers to **herem** as the negative consequence of disobedience on the "terrible day of the Lord."

III. **Herem** in the Kethubim

The Kethubim (Writings) contain a wide variety of literature (types, dates, quantity): everything from psalms to eschatological visions, narrative accounts to historiography, early to very late material. In this great quantity of written material there are six total occurrences of **herem**, four of which are used by the Chronicler.

KETHUBIM REFERENCE CHART - See Appendix I (cf. pp. 30f for usage details) (V-verb; N-noun; Literary forms: NA-Narrative; PPr-Prophetic Prose; GL-Genealogical List)

Ref.	Use	Lit Form	Ref.		Use	Lit Form	Ref.		Use	Lit Form
Dan 11.44	V 4	PPr	1Ch	2.7	N 1a	GL	2Ch	20.23	V 1a	NA
				4.41	V 1a	GL/NA		32.14	V 1a	NA
Ezr 10.8	V 5a/5b	NA								

Daniel, perhaps the latest book in the Kethubim, uses **herem** in prophetic prose to mean "destroy utterly" (Dan 11:44). It is related to the king of the North laying waste and doing **herem** to many (people). The "laying waste" (**samad**) parallels **herem** elsewhere (cf. Josh 7:12; 11:20; 2 Chr 20:23) and borders on wholesale slaughter (cf. discussion on Moabite stone, pp. 11f). This "doom" is followed by eschatological hope; "Michael the great prince" will enter the scene (Dan 10:13; 12:1).

Ezra 10:8 is part of a narrative with a proclamation (10:7) in which **herem** is the consequence (if...then). **Herem** of all the property or wealth of the person is parallel to the person being separated from the community of exiles (remnant community).[45] This usage of **herem** recalls the rules for handling booty, which were not applied consistently during wars, and especially during the conquest (Deut 2:34; 3:6; 7:26; 20:17; Jos 6-11). The real case law that applies is found in Deuteronomy 13:12-18, where a city of Israel is the object of **herem** because she has broken covenant by worshipping idols. The paradigm case is in Judges 21:8-12 when Jabesh-gilead does not respond to the call to assemble.

Chronicles uses **herem** twice in the literary context of a genealogical list (1 Chr 2:7; 4:41), and twice in narrative material (2 Chr 20:23; 32:14). Achan is identified in a genealogy by what he did with the booty (1 Chr 2:7). A story is told about how the sons of Simeon devoted the Meunim to **herem** and then settled in their place (1 Chr 4:41). This event is dated during Hezekiah's reign (ca. 715-687 B.C.E.). 2 Chronicles 20:23 is a most unusual event in which two of Judah's enemies destroy each other (**herem**)--Yahweh's miracle to save Judah. Imagery from the exodus era occurs in this story[46] and direct reference is made to Mount Sier (1 Chr 4:42). The final occurrence of **herem** is a narrative that is identical to 2 Kings 19:11 and Isaiah 37:11 (see above, pp. 17f).

IV. <u>Beyond the Old Testament</u>

The Old Testament uses **herem** with a number of different meanings. This diversity is reflected in the third century B.C.E. Greek translation of the Hebrew Bible, known as the Septuagint (LXX). In the Hebrew word index of the Septuagint eight page references occur for the noun form of **herem**; twenty-two page references for verb forms occur.[47] Not only is there no single term used in translating **herem** in Greek, but there are many alternatives. Further, the Septuagint is not consistent in its usage of Greek terms.[48]

Our comments on septuagintal usage must summarize some initial observations regarding this phase in the development of **herem** as a term in the Bible. Rebecca Yoder deals exclusively with the term **anathema** in only ten lines, where she addresses the septuagintal translation of **herem**.[49] Anathema is the term used more than any other single Greek term to translate **herem**, but if we compare all of the terms other than **anathema** that occur (21 total) we realize that **anathema** accounts for less than 40 percent of the total.[50] No doubt **anathema** is predominant, but, as the translators of the Septuagint recognized, it by no means covers the spectrum of meaning in **herem**. The New Testament only uses **anathema** and related root terms eleven times. According to the United Bible Societies' translation of the Hebrew New Testament, **anathema** is only translated by **herem** four times meaning "to curse" (1 Cor 12:3; 16:22; Gal 1:8,9).[51] This significantly narrows and alters its original OT range of meanings.

G. R. Driver makes a distinction between two Hebrew roots, determined by which passages refer to "devotion of people, as distinct from property, to God (**hrm**) and which refer to sheer extermination without any religious connotation (**hrm**)."[52] This distinction helps Driver classify certain Greek terms on that basis, distinguishing **anathematizo, anatithenai**, and **aphanizo** from **exolethruo, phronuo**, and **apokteino**.

The same Greek term is used in the Septuagint for **herem** and a parallel Hebrew term (Josh 10:35; 11:20, 21);[53] the opposite is the case in 2 Kings 19:11, Isaiah 37:11 and 2 Chronicles 32:14. These verses are identical in their use of **herem** in the Hebrew text, but the Septuagint uses three different Greek terms to translate it.[54] These observations are preliminary in nature. Even a surface observation indicates that the Septuagint translators understood the usage of **herem** in its diversity.[55]

Herem is used seven (possibly eight) times in three documents from the Qumran literature.[56] These occurrences provide a bridge from the Old Testament period through the intertestamental period and well

into the New Testament period. It is found in a
variety of literary forms (list of regulations on
behavior; casuistic law; rules governing behavior in
battle; list of consecrated objects). The two
predominant definitions of **herem** in the Qumran
literature are: 1. An object devoted to God, a
consecrated object; 2. Utterly destroy, utter
destruction, vow to destroy. There are several terms
used to parallel **herem** in this Qumran material that
are shared with the Old Testament.[57]

The usage of **herem** in the Qumran literature is
significant. It demonstrates a continuity with Old
Testament usage. It is used to mean "destroy utterly"
in the context of war narratives. It means
"consecrated object, or banned thing" as it is used in
the cultic setting. Both meanings are encompassed by
two basic ideas inherent in **herem**: Holiness and
covenant responsibility to God and the community. The
literary genres found in the Qumran literature carry
on the Old Testament tradition.

The remaining task for us is to consider the
transformation of the tradition. The history of
herem is woven into the ongoing dynamic history of
Israel. This transformation is observable in the Old
Testament and may be extrapolated beyond the Old
Testament.

Herem is a semitic term that is shared with other
ancient Near Eastern languages (cf. p. 17). Its
original meaning refers to that which is forbidden,
either because it is cursed and should be
exterminated, or because it is very holy.[58] This
broad meaning touches on how **herem** was carried out
in the Old Testament. **Herem** is used as part of
Israel's wars. It cannot be adequately understood if
discussed only as part of the "holy war" concept as
von Rad does (cf. p. 11). The pitfall of this
category, as it relates to the topic of
transformation, is that it imposes a legitimizing
function on **herem**. War can be justified if called
"holy war," and the act of **herem** becomes "necessary"
as the concluding cultic act in such a war. The war
needs **herem** to validate its "holy" status, and
herem can be carried out because such a war is
taking place. The New Testament era saw its share of
this type of war (i.e. Maccabean revolt; Zealot
uprisings; Bar Kochba revolt). Modern times witness
this when the Islamic Jihad is advocated. It also
rings true to the voice of civil religion in the
United States when the U.S. is viewed as God's tool

for **herem** in defending the "free world" from
atheistic communism as it spreads in many nations. To
free the term from the category of "holy war" means
that such a system of justifying one's warring is
dissociated from God's sanctioning.

The holiness motif is seen in the paradox of the
"holy" (**qodesh**) being bound together with the
"common, or profane" (**hol**).[59] **Herem** possesses
the qualities of being sacred <u>and</u> secular. This
combination is not surprising because the Israelites
did not separate the two as we do in a
post-enlightenment era of western thought. One
object, designated as **herem**, can be holy because it
is separated from common use (cf. Lev 27:21,28). It
can be profane if it is viewed as contaminating or
polluting to the holy (cf. Deut 7:26;13:18).[60] The
noun and verbal occurrences of **herem** are used both
ways. The transformation of the holiness motif
involves a narrowing of scope. In the Old Testament a
wide variety of objects may be consecrated as holy
herem (cf. Lev 27:21, 28; Num 18:14). Through the
intertestamental material and into the New Testament
this list is reduced to objects of value.[61] The
transformation of the "profane" motif also tends
toward a narrower focus. Whole cities (including men,
women, children, and other humans; cattle; and objects
like idols, gold, silver, and other metal booty) were
herem in the Old Testament (Num 21:1-3; Deut 2:34;
7:2, 26;13:16,18; Jos 6:17-21; 10-11; etc.). By the
period of the later prophets this view still exists,
and is in tension with the eschatological vision of
whom God will destroy utterly in the "day of the
Lord." Qumran retains this notion, especially in the
War Scroll. The New Testament, in its use of
anathema, speaks only of individuals who teach
things other than what Paul is teaching (Gal 1:8, 9),
or who say "Jesus be cursed" (1 Cor 12:3), or who have
"no love for the Lord" (1 Cor 16:22). These
individuals, who presumably are relating to the
Christian community, are to be considered accursed or
profane.

The act of destroying utterly means "to kill"
persons or other living beings in the Old Testament,
as legal punishment (Exod 22:19; Lev 27:29) and as
part of war (i.e. Deuteronomic History; Is 37:11 and
its parallels; Jer 50:21,26; Mic 4:13; Ezra 10:8; 1
Chr 4:41). This meaning is retained throughout the
Old Testament. In the New Testament the act is
transformed from killing in war (as the Christians had

no military) to treating a person as a cursed object
to be avoided, which leans toward the idea of legal
punishment (Exod 22:19; Lrv 27:29).[62] This is not a
paradigm for how **herem** is transformed in the New
Testament, it simply provides a link.[63] What can be
concluded regarding the transformation of the holiness
motif is that the scope of objects considered to be
herem is reduced. The act of **herem** is similarly
restricted more and more throughout time.

Summary and Conclusion

The foregoing observations offer a detailed
consideration of the primary biblical material. The
evidence suggests that **herem** is used in the Old
Testament with a variety of meanings and in a variety
of literary types. The biblical writers do not all
agree on how to use **herem**. This provides a
tension-filled mosaic picture, rather than a resolved
and uniform portrayal of how **herem** is used. Let us
summarize the ways in which **herem** is used as well as
mention some notions stimulated by the tension within
the biblical text itself. We must conclude with some
thoughts arising out of the transformation of **herem**.

The basic usages of **herem** in its verb and noun
forms are graphically outlined in Appendix I (pp.
29-31). The Torah sets the tone of diversity with its
usage of **herem** in a variety of literary types. The
law types (apodictic, casuistic, participial,
preaching of the law, and legal instruction) use
herem to mean an act of killing (as judicial
punishment, cultic sacrificial rite, or a part of
war). They also use it to signify an act of devoting
something to Yahweh such as banning an object, or
setting it apart from common use. **Herem** also means
an object devoted in such a fashion. The narrative
material uses **herem** as the act of vowing to destroy
or actually destroying the enemy in war.

The Nebi'im use five of the six verbal and all
three noun meanings for **herem**. The early prophets
use **herem** in narrative and oracle literature. The
verbal form either means "to destroy utterly" (or
not to do that), or the command to destroy utterly
in a context related to war.[64] The later prophets
use **herem** in several literary types (cf. Nebi'im
chart, p. 14). These references provide a bridge to
later material by using **herem** as the Torah and early
prophets did (cf. Isa 37:11; 43:28; Jer 50:21,26;
51:3; Ezek 44:29) and in new ways (Isa 34:5; Zech
14:11; Mal 4:24). The movement into prophesying

herem in eschatological terminology and the radical
prophetic criticism of Israel's people and
institutions focuses the presence of tension within
the biblical text.

The scant material provided in the Kethubim sheds
light on yet a later phase in Israel's history.
Daniel uses **herem** in prophetic prose as a prophecy
to destroy utterly (kill). Ezra 10:8 uses **herem** in
narrative literature, but as the legal consequence for
noncompliance to Ezra's proclamation. Chronicles uses
herem in narratives and genealogical lists to mean
"banned object" and "to destroy utterly" in war. This
late material retains the ideas of killing in war and
objects devoted or banned that was noted in the Torah.

The Bible does not use **herem** to mean just one
thing; nor does it use it in a single type of
literature. Diversity in the text not only provides a
broad background for understanding **herem**, but also
allows the reader to examine points at which the
writers differ and criticize each other. The most
obvious case in point is provided by the corpus of
Deuteronomic History and later prophets. The
Deuteronomist uses **herem** exclusively in connection
with war. In the book of Deuteronomy we have war
narratives which use **herem** and laws governing use of
herem in war. In the early prophets it means to
"destroy utterly" (or failure to do so) and the
command to "destroy utterly." This uniform conception
of **herem** as a war term with sacral/cultic
significance contrasts with the diversity of usage
found in the later prophets. The context of war is
still used, yet it becomes eschatological and there is
more diversity regarding the object of **herem**. These
later prophets view **herem** as God's tool to
discipline, judge, and redeem. The Deuteronomist
reflects a more nationalistic stance. Israel applies
herem to all unholy people, places, and objects.
Sennacherib, a non-Israelite, claims to have done
herem to all the nations, but ironically (and
consistent with Deuteronomic uniformity) fails to do
herem to Israel. The later prophets seem to take
issue with a smug nationalism that identifies Yahweh
with only Israel as a nation. They vent Yahweh's
frustration with Israel and Judah by prophesying
Israel to be the object of **herem**. Another aspect of
this development is the objectification of the term
herem as the term for God's act of utter destruction
(Isa 34:5; Zech 14:11; Mal 3:24). Simply put, these
differing usages of **herem** reflect divergence within

the biblical text which cannot be smoothed over. In fact these usages allow the reader to maintain a broader, more flexible understanding of **herem** throughout its development in the Old Testament. One stream of usage cannot be traced into the New Testament and definitely associated to a single usage there.

The primitive and less morally palatable usage of **herem** to mean "utter destruction" of persons is present in the Bible. God <u>did</u> command Israel to do "utter destruction," according to the text (cf. parallels to **herem** in Appendix I, pp. 29-31). At the same time **herem** has a broader meaning than to destroy in war. The existence of these diverse meanings must be acknowledged and not explained away. That Yahweh is a warrior does not negate the fact that Jesus is the Prince of Peace. To digress into the area of hermeneutics and theological rationalizations of the peace position would take us beyond the scope of this paper. Let us say in brief that **herem** does not exclusively address the topic of war and peace in the Bible. Yahweh's command to obedience in all things, including **herem**, means that it is God who is sovereign over all things. Only Yahweh has the power and right to give and take life.

Central to the usage of **herem** in the Old Testament is holiness. **Herem** has the two-fold character containing the diametrically opposed ideas of the holy (**qodesh**) and the profane (**hol**). Holiness is the key to the sacral/cultic idea in **herem**. Holiness provides impetus to discern between uses of **herem**. Another core concept is obedience to God within the covenant community. This relationship to other persons under Yahweh's lordship defines what faithfulness is, what justice means, and who is or is not part of the covenant community.

The transformation of **herem** beyond the Old Testament is difficult to pinpoint. One notion to consider is that **herem** takes on a narrower meaning as a verb. It becomes restricted to eschatological wars, since military expeditions are not part of Christian life in the New Testament. Another notion is that **herem** as a noun is taking on the limited twofold sense of: 1. Consecrated object; 2. Something or someone to be considered profane or cursed. The first meaning applies to cultic offerings or sacred devoted objects. The second meaning refers to judging within the community of faith between the sacred and profane. It may in this usage relate to the process of discipline in the church.

Herem in the Old Testament partakes of its larger diversity. This critical reflection on the meaning and usage of **herem** in the Bible reveals no uniformity. The term is rooted in the ancient traditions of Israel (note especially the connections to the exodus event), but is not a term exclusive to the Hebrew language. In the Hebrew Bible, though, Yahweh is the sovereign God in control of defining and commanding **herem**. It is within the tradition of faithfulness to Yahweh that **herem** takes on a meaning other than simply exterminating the enemy in war. **Herem** is both a nationalistic weapon and the tool for chastizing God's people. In scanning the long-term transformation of **herem** we note an unexpected connection with Yahweh's desire to redeem God's people. In the light of that **go'el** tradition we find Jesus coming as redeemer and judge of all creation. It may be time to reflect back on **herem** in light of the Jesus event.

Appendix I

The following chart provides a synopsis of how **herem** is used in the primary material. The separate verb and noun charts tabulate each occurrence of **herem** under several significant categories. These charts allow the reader to observe graphically the similarities and differences, primary and secondary usages, and the boundaries of the concept conveyed by the term.

A few words explaining the symbols on the chart are in order. The + and - deal with the sense in which the text uses **herem** as a noun. The <- symbol indicates that the text uses the category marked "x", but the context points to the <- category as the implicit agent. Brackets [] are used to identify occurrences that could be listed under more than one usage. Some references have more than one occurrence of the root חרם . Such cases are noted with a lower case letter in parentheses following the reference (i.e. Josh 7:13(b)). All verb forms are Hip'il except where the reference is followed by (Ho). This signifies that these references use the Hop'al form of the verb.

ḤEREM USAGE CHART

Verb Categories

AGENT	OBJECT	MEANS
1. Yahweh	1. Non-Israelites	1. War
2. Israel-Nation	2. Israelites	2. Sacrifice
3. Israel-Individuals	3. Animals	3. Devoting
4. Other Nation(s)	4. City, Town	4. Unclear
5. Other Individuals	5. Metals, Objects	
6. Undefined	6. Lands, Nations	

Noun Categories

TYPE OF LITERATURE		GRAMMATICAL USE
1. Narrative	6. Oracle	1. Nominative
2. Law	7. Genealogical list	2. Accusative
3. Prophetic Prose	8. Epic, Saga	3. Dative
4. Prophetic Poetry	+ = Positive	4. Genitive
5. Lament	- = Negative	

Context (Shared Category)

1. War	5. Divine Judgment	9. Sacral Vow
2. Civil War	6. Law	10. Exodus
3. Preparing For War	7. Covenant Making	11. Genealogy
4. Labor List	8. Cultic	

Appendix I Cont.

VERB FORMS

USAGE	REFERENCES	AGENT 1 2 3 4 5 6	OBJECT 1 2 3 4 5 6	MEANS 1 2 3 4	CONTEXT 1 - 11	Parallel Terms
1a. Utterly	Nu 21.3	x	x	x	3,9	
Destroy	Dt 2.34	x	x x	x	1	Raq-šᵉlālāh
	3.6(2x)	x	x x	x	1	
	Jos 2.10	x	x	x	1	
	6.21	x	x x x	x	1	Ḥereb
	8.26	x	x	x	1	
	10.1	x	x	x	1	
	10.28	<-x	x	x	1	Ḥereb;Nākāh
	10.35	<-x	x	x	1	Ḥereb;Nākāh
	10.37	<-x	x x	x	1	Ḥereb;Nākāh
	10.39	x	x	x	1	Ḥereb;Nākāh
	10.40	<-x	x	x	1	Nākāh
	11.11	x	x	x	1	Ḥereb;Nākāh
	11.12	<-x	x x	x	1	Ḥereb;Nākāh
	11.20	x	x	x	1	Šāmad
	11.21	<-x	x x	x	1	Kārāt;Hašālā
	Jud 1.17	x	x	x	1	Nakah
	21.11	x	x	x	3	
	1Sa 15.8	<-x	x	x	1	
	15.9(a)	x	x	x	1	Ḥereb
	15.15	x	x	x	1	Zābaḥ
	15.20	x	x	x	1	Bᵉderek
*2Ki	19.11	x		x x	1	
*Is	37.11	x		x x	1	
*Identical	1Ch 4.41	x	x	x	1	Nākāh
Verses	2Ch 20.23	x	x	x	1	Šāmad;Kālāh
*	32.14	x		x x	1	
1b. Not Utterly						
Destroy	1Sa 15.9(b)	x	x	x	1	
	1Ki 9.21	x	x	x	1,4	Kālāh
2 Command to	[Dt 7.2(2x)]	x	x	x	6	Nākāh
Utterly	Jos 6.18	(x)x	(x) x	x x	3	
Destroy	1Sa 15.3	x	x x	x	3	Nākāh;Môt
	15.18	x	x	x	3	Kālāh;Lāham
	[Jer 50.21]	x	x	x	5	Ḥereb
	[50.26]	x		x x	5	
	[51.3]	x x		x x	5	
3 Oath to Utterly						
Destroy	Nu 21.2	x	x	x	3,9	
4 Prophecy to	Is 34.2	x	x x	x	5	Tābaḥ
Utterly	Jer 25.9	x	x x x x	x	5	
Destroy	[50.21]	x	x	x	5	
	[50.26]	x		x x	5	
	[51.3]	x x		x x	5	
	Mic 4.13	x	x	x	1	Šāmad
	Dan 11.44	x		x x	1	

Appendix I Cont.

	References	1	2	3	4	5	6	7	+ or -	1	2	3	4	Context	
5a. Law to	Ex 22.19(Ho)	x			x	x							x	6,8	Lo'-Ḥāyāh;Môt
Utterly	Lv 27.29(Ho)		x	x	x								x	6,9	Zābaḥ
Destroy	[Dt 7.2(2x)]	x			x						x			6	Nākāh
	13.16	x								x	x	x	x x	2,6	Ḥereb;Nākāh
	20.17(2x)	x			x		x				x			6	
	[Ezr 10.8(Ho)]	x	x				x					x		7,9	
5b. Law to	Lv 27.28	x			x	x						x		9	
Set Apart	[Ezr 10.8(Ho)]	x	x				x					x		7,9	
6 Divide	Is 11.15	x					x						x	10	Nākāh

NOUN FORMS

USAGE	REFERENCES	TYPE OF LITERATURE							+ or -	GRAMMATICAL USE				CONTEXT	
		1	2	3	4	5	6	7		1	2	3	4	1 – 11	
1. Objects															
a. Devoted	Dt 13.18	x							–	x				6	
to be	Jos 6.17	x							–	x				3	
Destroyed	[6.18(a)]	x							–			x		3	
	[6.18(b)]	x							–			x		3	
	7.1(a)	x							–		x			3	
	7.1(b)	x							–			x		3	
	7.11	x							–			x		3	
	7.12(b)		(x)	x					–		x			5	Šāmad
	[7.13(a)]			x					–	x				5	
	7.13(b)			x					–		x			5	Qaḏōš
	[7.15]			x					–			x		5	
	[22.20]	x							–			x		1,7	
	1Sa 15.21	x							–			x		1	Zābaḥ
	1Ch 2.7					x			–			x		11	
b. Which	Dt 7.26(a)	x							–	x				6	
Pollute	7.26(b)	x							–	x				6	
(Profane)	[Jos 6.18(a)]	x							–			x		3	
	[6.18(b)]	x							–			x		3	
	[7.13(a)]			x					–	x				5	Qaḏōš
	[7.15]			x					–			x		5	
	[22.20]	x							–			x		1,7	
c. Set Apart	Lv 27.21	x							+				x	6,8,9	Qaḏōš
for Yahweh	27.28(a)	x							+	x				6,8,9	Qaḏōš
(Holy)	27.28(b)	x							+	x				6,8,9	Qaḏōš
	Nu 18.14	x							+	x				6,8,9	
	Ezk 44.29	(x)	x						+	x				6,8,9	
2 Persons	Lv 27.29	x							–	x				6,8,9	
Devoted to	Jos 6.18(c)	x							–		x			3	Ga'al;Mô
be Destroyed	7.12(a)		(x)	x					–	x				5	Šāmad
	1Ki 20.42	x							–			x		5	Šāmad
	Is 43.28			x					–			x		5	
3 The Act of	Is 34.5				x	(x)			–			x		5	Qaḏōš
Destroying	Zec 14.11			x					+	x				5	
	Mal 3.24				x	(x)			–			x		5	

Appendix II

The Ban in Mari Material
   "The Ban - a peculiar expression at Mari, **asakkam akalum** (lit. 'to eat the asakku'), refers to the infringement of a taboo or the profaning of something revered, and may be a loan translation of some West Semitic concept paralleling that of the biblical ban (**herem**). The asakku of a particular deity, and/or king is frequently invoked in penalty clauses of contracts, in oaths, and in royal decrees as the sacrosanct and inviolable element. The closest parallel between Mari and the biblical practice is in the imposition of the ban on spoils of war (cf., eg., the Achan incident, Joshua 7). However, whereas the biblical ban functioned on a purely religious plane (whatever was banned was exclusively God's), the taboo at Mari was applicable also on a human level, and its infringement there, though theoretically still considered a capital offense, was expiated by payment of a simple fine."

Quoted from, Abraham Malamat, "Mari," Encyclopedia Judaica, Vol. 11, p. 987.

1.   This form is used throughout the paper to represent the Hebrew cognate חרם .

2.   This phrase is taken from John H. Yoder. It means "reading the text for what it is about, asking what are its own questions and concerns" (Yoder's introduction to Millard Lind's book, Yahweh is a Warrior [Scottdale: Herald Press, 1980], p. 19). It is a way of allowing the text to speak, unrestricted by the reader.

3.   W. D. Davies, "Law in the Old Testament," The Interpreter's Dictionary of the Bible (New York: Abingdon Press, 1962), III, 77-95. See also, Millard C. Lind, "Law in the Old Testament," The Bible and the Law, ed. Willard M. Swartley (Elkhart: Institute of Mennonite Studies, 1982), 9-41.

4.   Exodus 21:12 begins with a consonantal form that is ambiguous without vowel pointing. It may be a hip'il participle or a noun. Taken as a participle, this verse would signal the beginning of a participial law section. Taken as a noun, verses 12-14 would be part of the casuistic law section. We accept v 12 as participial, but even if only vv 15-17 are considered participial, we still have a break in the casuistic law section. See especially Hans Jochen Boecker, Law and the Administration of Justice in the Old Testament and Ancient East, trans. Jeremy Moiser (Minneapolis: Augsburg Publishing House, 1980), 194-97.

5.   This has been observed by various scholars. See especially Rifat Sonsino, Motive Clauses in Hebrew Law: Biblical Forms and Near Eastern Parallels (Chico, CA: Scholars Press, 1980).

6.   See note 4 for a discussion regarding inclusion of Exodus 21:12-14 here.

7.   Exodus 21:12-17 contains participial law regarding relations between people (striking a person, or a parent; stealing a person; cursing a parent). Exodus 22:17-19 addresses situations where persons are violating order or relationship with God (sorcery; lying with a beast; sacrificing to idols).

8.   All references correspond with the Hebrew text of Biblia Hebraica Stuttgartensia (Stuttgart: Deutsche Bibelstiftung, 1977). These references may

differ from RSV references, as in Exodus 22:19 which
is 22:20 in the RSV.

9.   Otto Eissfeldt, The Old Testament: An
Introduction, trans. Peter R. Ackroyd (New York:
Harper & Row Publishers, 1965), 212-19.   He argues to
call it "B" while others give it different sigla, yet
they agree that it is independent.

10.   See Otto Eissfeldt, ibid., 191-99; Georg
Fohrer, Introduction to the Old Testament
(Nashville: Abingdon, 1968), 159-65 argues for a
third early stratum, apart from J and E, which he
calls the "Nomadic Source Stratum" (N).   This differs
from Eissfeldt's "Lay Source" (L) basically in the way
he perceives the source as a whole.   The material
assigned to this source by the two authors corresponds
for the most part.

11.   Gerhard von Rad, Studies in Deuteronomy,
trans. David Stalker (London: SCM Press, Ltd., 1948),
47-49.   Also see his basic work, Der heilige Krieg im
alten Israel (Gottingen: Vandenhoeck and Ruprecht,
1950).

12.   von Rad, Deuteronomny, trans. Dorothea
Barton, OT Library Series (Philadelphia: Westminster
Press, 1966), V, 43-44.

13.   von Rad, Studies in Deuteronomy, 48-49.

14.   Rudolf Smend, Yahweh War and Tribal
Confederation, trans. Max Gray Rogers (Nashville:
Abingdon Press, 1970).

15.   Manfred Weippert, "'Heiliger Krieg' in Israel
und Assyrien: Kritische Anmerkungen zu Gerhard von
Rads Konzept des 'Heiligen Krieges im alten Israel',"
Zeitschrift fur die alttestamentliche Wissenschaft
84(1972), 485.

16.   Peter C. Craige, The Problem of War in the
Old Testament (Grand Rapids: Wm. B. Eerdmans, 1978),
48-49.

17.   Peter C. Craige, The Book of Deuteronomy,
NICOT (Grand Rapids: Wm. B. Eerdmans, 1976), 177.

18.   Casuistic law (**ki**...**'im**) predominates the chapter, but vv 16-18 seem to take on the emphatic style of apodictic law (**raq**) with motive clauses (**aser**).

19.   Craige, Deuteronomy, 58. This connects the discussion with the biblical paradigm for war, i.e. via Yahweh's miracle. It also puts **herem** in the context of conquest. Beyond this are hints that foretell the Deuteronomist's position throughout the early prophetic material which is in tension with the later prophetic usage of **herem** (cf. below, p. 20).

28.   This story parallels the crossing of the Reed Sea narrative (Exod 14). It also consists of covenant-making and cultic practices (i.e. handling the ark of the covenant; circumcision of males). This material seems out of place in the Jericho narrative sequence, yet very much related to the importance of the covenant and "miracle" in Israel's history to this point and the anticipated conquest.

21.   Patrick D. Miller, "God the Warrior," Interpretation 19(1965), 43. He follows von Rad's understanding of the theological reinterpretation found in Deuteronomy.

22.   Norman Gottwald, "'Holy War' in Deuteronomy: Analysis and Critique," Review and Expositor 61(1964), 304.

23.   Norman Gottwald, The Tribes of Yahweh (Maryknoll, NY: Orbis Books, 1979), 547f.

24.   George Mendenhall, "The Hebrew Conquest of Palestine," The Biblical Archaeologist 25(1963), 73.

25.   The very process of writing Israel's history meant an interpretation of the events that occurred. This process of transmitting the history, although interpreting the events in light of faith in Yahweh, was based on actual experiences.

26.   Gottwald, Tribes, 547f. See also an unpublished paper by Anne Crawford, " חרם : A Resistance to the Oppressive Kingship of the Canaanite City-State?," 1983. She highlights the inconsistent application of **herem** to booty in the Old Testament.

27.   Does the use of **herem** in Israel's history reflect an attempt to institute economic equality? The statute that men of war not hoard booty was a way to enforce such equality. The problem with this idea arises in the Mari materials when **asakku** is prohibited by the <u>state</u> so the king could consolidate the wealth. In the Mesha Stele, the Moabite god Chemosh is given the booty and sacrifice of living things. Again, the role of the king as the god's ordained representative provides the basis for understanding **herem** in this Moabite stone. The king, as the god's representative, was recipient of all the booty. This meant the consolidation of wealth in the hands of the ruling class or the existing oppressive state system. The way that Israel avoids this natural trap of a person or a class of people hoarding the booty from war is to redefine the religious-political structure of their society. They did not need to develop a communistic state or societal structure to guarantee people a fair share of the booty. They simply had to behave according to the nature and example of Yahweh. Yahweh was liberator of the oppressed people in Egypt. The historical precedent of the exodus revealed to the people how God acts. That meant Yahweh would not oppress or deal with people unfairly. The natural conclusion for the Hebrew people was that they could not act that way and stay in Yahweh's favor. This God was the only God, needing no divine personification in the role of king to enforce divine law. Therefore, Israel had no king to whom all booty went. The trap of hoarding was avoided by calling the people to obedience and by not instituting kingship. As time passed Israel chose kingship, but even then it was an institution that was understood differently within Israel than outside of Israel. It was a monarchy, yes, but one open to God's criticism and judgment through the prophets. It was not in control of the cultic institutions either.

The conclusion from this note is that regardless of the method of conquering (annihilation, infiltration, or revolt) the booty was purposefully kept from being hoarded and unequally distributed. The contention that **herem** relates to Israel's efforts at establishing an equitable socio-economic system has <u>some</u> credence. It should not be pushed too far that **herem** was the <u>means</u> for establishing economic equality.

28. Mendenhall, ibid. The article is based on the observation that such widespread and absolute destruction is not supported by archaeological evidence. The redefinition of "Hebrew" helps answer the question of how Canaanites survived such utter destruction (Josh 2; 6-11) and why they posed such a threat to Israel throughout its existence. It is consistent with the "local" nature of the overthrow of Palestine city-states at that time.

29. See the many cross references in an English Bible. Note the narratives, laws about war, the instance of a vow (Num 21:1-3), and Israel itself becoming **herem** (Deut 13:16).

30. Joshua 3-5 interrupts the Jericho narrative (2-6). Joshua 9, the treaty with the Gibeonites, interrupts the **herem** accounts of conquest (8-11). Joshua 12-21 is a block of material with lists of kings and cities defeated and inheritance allotments. These chapters even have short narrative and law preaching sections that infringe on the orderly account of inheritances (14:6-14; 15:13-19; 17:3-5, 14-18; 18:2-10; 20:1-9). Joshua 23-24 are an epilogue focusing on the main character of the book, Joshua. This epilogue reemphasizes the themes of Yahweh's history of saving events and covenant renewal at Shechem. The book of Judges is much more open about the existence of Canaanites in Palestine than is suggested by Joshua. 1 Samuel has pro and con versions regarding the annointing of Saul. Finally, 2 Kings 19:11 is paralleled in Isaiah 37:11 and 2 Chronicles 32:14, revealing dependence on or sharing of other sources.

31. Judges may be an earlier compilation of material that utilized independent stories regarding Israel's struggle to survive in Palestine after the conquest. It may be that the Deuteronomist made editorial additions to the beginning and end of his own compilation so that the larger Deuteronomic History would have continuity. **Herem** is part of a literary device (inclusion) that hooks this book to what preceded (conquest), and to what follows (kingship). In either case **herem** seems to be a term used early in Israel's history, yet not exclusively in religious wars of conquest.

32. Chapters 1-7 are a transition from Judges to the institution of a prophet as God's mouthpiece. Chapters 8-14 are the record of how Israel chose to institute kingship in its social structure. Saul's compliance with Canaanite patterns of kingship behavior, and his failure to obey Yahweh in carrying out **herem** cause Yahweh to reject him as annointed king over Israel (1 Sam 15:34-16:1). After 1 Samuel 15, the downfall of Saul, and rise of David and David's kingship are the focus. **Herem** is absent from this material even though many military engagements are recorded.

33. This corresponds to Mendenhall's peasant revolt model of the conquest. It is a criticism of Israel's faithfulness to **herem** during the conquest. It also is a criticism of the institution of kingship in as much as such forced slavery is the polar opposite of what the "Hebrews" were trying to accomplish in their conquest of Palestine (see Mendenhall, ibid., 71f for his broader definition of "Hebrew"). The biblical text is quick to point out that Solomon did not make slaves of the people of Israel (1 Kgs 9:22). This is "pro-kingship" and **herem** makes sense in the southern tradition of material if used this way.

34. James B. Pritchard, Ancient Near Eastern Texts, 3rd ed. (Princeton: Princeton University Press, 1969), 320.

35. Abraham Malamat, "The Ban in Mari and in the Bible," Mari and the Bible (Jerusalem: Hebrew University, 1975), 57. See also his note, "The Ban in the Old Testament and at Mari," The Biblical Archaeologist 47(1984), 103.

36. Gottwald, Tribes, 545-46. Malamat makes an assumption that there is a connection between Mari and the "semi-nomadic" legal practices prior to Israelite conquest of Canaan. Gottwald, and Mendenhall (ibid., 67-69) criticize the assumption made about semi-nomadic tribes. The proper understanding is rather a stigma put on these unsanctioned behaviors. The key to the Mari documents' contribution to our understanding of **herem** is the direct association between the office and person of the king, as well as the god(s), and the military taboo sanctions. In Mari the king is benefactor of **asakku** sanctions because of his power base, and this results in a concentration

of wealth. In Israel there is no human king to amass
wealth when **herem** is commanded. Saul misuses the
practice of **herem** and loses his position of favor as
a result. **Herem** is not used in military exploits by
Israel subsequent to Saul's failure to obey and so it
is not used as a religiously sanctioned manipulation
of people or wealth by a king.

37. Gottwald, "'Holy War' in Deuteronomy:
Analysis and Critique," Review and Expositor
61(1964), 301. This is also noted by Patrick D.
Miller, The Divine Warrior in Early Israel, Harvard
Semitic Monographs, 5 (Cambridge: Harvard Univ.
Press, 1973), 45. Miller sees a parallel to **rit**
"satiation" (cf. Isa 34:2, 5).

38. This is known as "First Isaiah." Chapters
40-55 constitute "Deutero-Isaiah" and 56-66 are
considered "Trito-Isaiah." The critical division of
Isaiah into these sections has been called into
question and the dates of the latter two sections are
a matter of guesswork. The only reference to **herem**
other than in "First Isaiah" is found in Isaiah 43:28.
This occurrence reflects law court imagery of an
earlier era (cf. Isa 1:18; Hos 4:1-4; 12:2; Mic 6).
The context assumes the Babylonian exile and supplies
a link in the continuum of Israel's history.

39. Gerhard von Rad, "The Origin of the concept of
the Day of Yahweh," Journal of Semitic Studies
4(1959), 97-108. I have already addressed the topic
of holy war, see above pp. 11-13. As for the "day of
Yahweh" some connections with the use of **herem** as
the end of this "day" can be made, but **herem** cannot
be limited **herem** to this meaning. Nor can the
imagery of the "day" be so definitively concluded by
the event of **herem**. The end of the "day" is too
often other than **herem** to make such a restricting
conclusion.

40. G. R. Driver, "Hebrew Homonyms," Supplement
to Vetus Testamentum (Leiden: E. J. Brill, 1967),
XVI, 59. Here Driver argues for a distinction between
hrm and **hrm** as separate roots which have been
considered the same. His argument points out cases
where confusing texts can be understood more clearly
if terms are assigned to the correct root. Thus, he
translates "The Lord shall divine i.e. open a way
through the tongue of the Egyptian sea," rather than

"the Lord shall destroy utterly..." The dividing of
the sea refers back to the exodus event and projects
that as the new hope for the remnant people. There is
no utter destruction of people at all as in the "holy
war" concept.

41. This comes the closest to the usage of **herem**
in the Moabite stone, cf. above p. 21.

42. This oracle is dated in Jer 25:1 (ca 609
B.C.E.). This was the end of an era of renewed hope
under Josiah. The law had been rediscovered
(connected with Deut 12-26) and sparked a religious
revival. Jeremiah reflects the self-criticism of the
prophets of old.

43. I cannot determine the direction of borrowing
here. The Torah material is of an earlier oral
tradition, regardless of when it was finally compiled.
Ezekiel's vision makes most sense as the absolutizing
of earlier religious ideals about the temple. The
date of Ezekiel (ca 593-571 B.C.E.) raises the
possibility that the cycle went the opposite
direction, with the prophet receiving these ordinances
in a vision and recording them. The record of the
vision eventually may have been incorporated into
already existing Torah material during a later
editorial revision of the entire collected corpus.
The evidence could be argued either way. We are
inclined to agree with the primacy of the Torah
material. The interesting note aside from this
literary question is that the source for these
ordinances in the Torah is tradition P. This source
is dated in the sixth century by some. The dependence
of Ezekiel on this material may be due to his role as
priest and the availability of this source in the
period of exile in Babylon.

44. A full treatment of this idea is given by Paul
D. Hanson, The Dawn of the Apocalyptic
(Philadelphia: Fortress Press, 1975). At tension
here are the cosmic visionary ideas found in the royal
Jerusalem cult and the realistic, almost programmed,
perspective of promise and fulfillment developed by
the Deuteronomist. Hanson argues that Second Isaiah
raised this dialectic to a high tension. "Primordial
event, historical past, and future salvation are all
brought together into one dynamic tension-filled unity
which permits Yahweh neither to be reduced to the

one-dimensional historicizing of the Deuteronomic History nor to escape into the timelessness of myth" (p. 25). The prophet is able to provide a balance in the biblical text. There are multiple perspectives in the text and the prophets bring these strains into focus by providing necessary criticism of current dogmatism. The prophetic message goes its own direction, yet it stands out as an intra-biblical check on subsequent smoothing and synthesis of the history.

45. This translation is contrary to the RSV which misleadingly translates that the person will be "banned." **Herem** is usually translated "ban" and here it is property that is being "banned."

46. 2 Chronicles 20:15-17, esp. v 17, "You will not need to fight in this battle; take your position, stand still, and see the victory of the Lord on your behalf..." reiterates Exodus 14:13-14, "Fear not, stand firm, and see the salvation of the Lord, which he will work for you today... The Lord will fight for you, and you only have to be still." The use of **herem** in this "miracle" event may be the Chronicler's way of relating this later history to the long tradition of Israel which acknowledges Yahweh as warrior. See Lind, Yahweh is a Warrior, 48-64.

47. E. Hatch & H. A. Redpath, eds., A Concordance to the Septuagint (Oxford: N.P., 1947).

48. Either there was great flexibility of the Greek terms which embodied the meaning of **herem**, or there was a lot of confusion about what **herem** meant. The LXX changes the Hebrew text at times (note the textual variants), or various LXX texts offer divergent Greek terms for one text. The variety of Greek terms points to the span of nuance which exists in **herem** as it is used in the Hebrew text.

49. Rebecca Yoder, "Old Testament Cherem and New Testament Sentences of Holy Law," Occasional Papers (Elkhart: Institute of Mennonite Studies, 1980), 1, 23.

50. See E. Hatch & H. A. Redpath, ibid., for the overwhelming statistics. It is difficult to be precise with numbers of occurrences assigned to each Greek term because Hatch and Redpath list Greek roots

together and there are variant readings between the
Hebrew text used today and that which was available at
the time when their concordance was compiled. Roughly
speaking, **anathema** is used 30-32 times for the
eighty occurrences of **herem** in the Hebrew text.
Other terms are used for the remaining 47-49
occurrences. The LXX does not translate Joshua 8:26,
thus the total possible is 79 rather than 80.

51. Hebrew New Testament (Israel: United Bible
Societies, 1983).

52. G. R. Driver, ibid., 57. See my discussion
of the value of assigning terms to the proper root
based on Driver's distinction above, footnote 40.
Religious and non-religious may not be the most
accurate categories. Israel's entire life was
permeated with religion, as was the case in the
ancient Near East generally. It would be difficult to
make this religious-non-religious distinction in the
context of the eastern mentality. I would retain the
distinction, but rather view the categories as
sacral/cultic and non-sacral/cultic or
religio-political and religio-economic or social.

53. Joshua 10:35 - **herem** and **nakah** are both
translated by **phoneuein**. This is the only time this
Greek term is used to translate **herem**. Joshua 11:20
- **herem** and **samad** are both translated by
exolethreuein. Joshua 11:21 - **herem** and **karat**
are both translated by **exolethreuein**.

54. 2 Kings 19:11 - **anathematizein**; Isaiah 37:11
- **apolluein**; 2 Chronicles 32:14 - **exolethruein**.

55. The exactness and precision of the Greek
language allowed them to deal with different nuances
of meaning by using different terms. These many terms
must be followed through the LXX, the Apocrypha, and
into the New Testament. When this larger scale
evaluation of Greek terms is completed, then the broad
scope of meaning embodied in **herem** can be traced
beyond its Old Testament origins.

56. Damascus Document (CDC) 6:15; 9:1; 16:15; War
Scroll (DSW) 9:7; 18:5; Copper Scroll (3Q15) 9:10(?);
9:16; 11:7.

57. See Appendix I (pp. 29–31) for parallels to the Old Testament occurrences. **Qodesh** (holy) is found near CDC 6:15 (6:1, 18, 20) and near CDC 16:15 (16:14, 16, 17). **Mot** (die) is found near CDC 9:1 (9:6) and is used similarly to Old Testament participial law consequences (Ex 21:12–17; 22:17–19). **Samad** (destroy) and **kalah** (cut off, annihilate) occur near CDC 9:7 (9:5, 6). **Salal** (booty, spoil) is used near CDC 6:15 (6:16).

58. C. Brekelmans, " חרם heroem Bann," Theologisches Handworterbuch zum Alten Testament, eds. Ernst Jenni and Claus Westermann (Munchen: Chr. Kaiser Verlag, 1971), 2, 635. This article gives a good, brief review of the usage of **herem** (unfortunately only in German).

59. Norman H. Snaith, The Distinctive Ideas of the Old Testament (London: The Epworth Press, 1944), 32–34.

60. **Herem** is similar to "shame" in this dual capacity. When a person has shame, that means he/she knows what is disgraceful or dishonorable and avoids such behavior. A person can be shameful because of improper behavior, incompetence, etc. Both the positive and negative are contained in this one term.

61. See especially the Copper Scroll (3Q15) occurrences of **herem** (see footnote 56). **Herem** is moving toward being silver and gold objects restricted to the cultic setting. This may suggest movement toward monetary equivalents for devoted objects. The change goes along with the restrictions of repressive empires under which the Jewish people lived, and evolution of Jewish religious practice. In Christian religious practice, things devoted to God were for the benefit of the community of believers (cf. Acts 4:32–5:11).

62. This is based on the usage of **anathema** in the New Testament cited above, p. 22, see footnote 51. It must be re-emphasized that this is a touchstone in looking at transformations. **Anathema** is not the only Greek term used to translate **herem**, see above pp. 22f. This usage in the New Testament needs to be noted, but it must not be absolutized as the singular definitive way **herem** is transformed in New Testament usage. It is good logic to say that this use of

anathema in the New Testament derives from the use
of herem in the Old Testament. It is poor logic
to assume the converse to be true. Herem cannot
logically be funneled into this one narrow usage of
one of the many Greek terms used to translate herem.

63. This statement basically agrees with the
argument of Marlin Jeschke's book, Discipling the
Brother (Scottdale: Herald Press, 1972). It calls
into question the sequence of argument provided by
Rebecca Yoder, ibid., 23-26. Her conclusion is that
"the 'anathema' functions for the church's
preservation, as the Deuteronomist had long before
interpreted the meaning of Old Testament holy war
'herem'" (Yoder, 28). The logic leading up to this
conclusion, which connects herem so closely with
anathema, is faulty (see note 62). Her connection
between the Achan event in Joshua 7 and the story of
Ananias and Sapphira (Acts 5:1-11) is "clear"
(Yoder, p. 23). Both cases deal with discipline
within the community of faith, but how far can the
Achan incident be pushed in its connection of herem
to New Testament church discipline? There is quite a
jump from destruction of an entire family with all its
possessions, to the death of two individuals, to
excommunication from the community of faith and no
physical death whatsoever. We agree that discipline
within the community of faith is the central point,
but the use of herem in Joshua 7 and absence of
parallel Greek terms in Acts 5:1-11 makes the
connection less than "substantial."

65. See Appendix I, pp. 20-31. Contexts 1, 2, and
3 are directly related to war. Context 4 (1 Kgs 9:21)
relates herem itself to war. Context 5 is judgment
made based upon what happened in the war context.

VIOLENCE AND THE SACRED SCAPEGOAT

Edmund Pries

I. Introduction

This paper is not so much a study of a particular topic as it is an attempt at understanding a theme as it was progressively developed by two scholarly authors. René Girard's Violence and the Sacred (Baltimore: Johns Hopkins University Press, 1977) forms the philosophical and theoretical basis for Raymund Schwager's biblical study Brauchen wir einen Sündenbock? Gewalt und Erlösung in den Biblischen Schriften (München: Kösel-Verlag, 1978), which means Do we need a Scapegoat? Violence and Redemption in the Biblical Writings.

In his book Girard attempts to show the vital and integral relation between violence and sacred ritual (all religion), as it is expressed primarily through sacrifice. His perspective is one of anthropology, literary analysis, and psychoanalysis. Anthropologically, Girard draws on a wide range of 'primitive' tribal religions, from the monarchies of Africa to the tribes of Latin America, as well as on the structural similarities between modern societies and ancient religious societies. Theology enters the discussion only in the form of philosophy of religion--no mention is ever made of Christianity. The exclusion of Christianity is with purpose; in later articles Girard explains that he considers the Christ Way as lying outside the normal philosophy of religion. Girard's literary analysis includes primarily all the ancient Greek tragedies with some Shakespeare, Milton, Goethe, etc. added. In the area of psychoanalysis, Girard critiques quite brilliantly the theses of Freud and his followers.

Schwager bases his biblical study upon the thesis of Girard. After outlining Girard's thinking and his own understanding of it, Schwager traces the theme of violence through the Old and New Testament, showing that Christ was the necessary scapegoat who took the violence of all people upon himself. By responding contrary to the law of violence and universally absorbing all of the hostility, Christ broke free from those bonds and enables his followers to do the same.

This paper will attempt a comprehensive summary of Girard's and Schwager's scholarship and then draw some

conclusions as to the implications of their thought
for Anabaptist peace understandings.

II. Violence and the Sacred
   A. Introduction
     Girard believes that "...violence and the sacred
are one and the same thing" (G:262) for "...the
operations of violence and the sacred are ultimately
the same process" (G:258). Violence finds its refuge
in the sacred through sacrifice, yet it is the
function of sacrifice "to quell violence in the
community and to prevent conflicts from erupting"
(G:14). This, according to Girard, is what religion's
role essentially is, namely to save a community from
the destructive effects of violence by deflecting the
violence onto a surrogate victim who is then
sacrificed according to religious ritual. Thus the
peace and security of the community is restored.
     Throughout his book Girard attempts to portray the
link between violence and religion (sacrifice and
sacrificial ritual) as an inseparable bond that exists
in all communities that will to survive. The central
problem in all communities is violence--all other
evils and problems are hinged on this central ill. It
is religion's task to deal with this source of evils;
thus violence and the sacred are the two foci of all
societies--one the evil, the other the antidote. As
Schwager says of Girard's view of the sacred, "Sacred
is for him that which stands in relation to violence
in its original form, that which is oriented to remind
one of it, and that which threatens to absolve a new
crisis" (S:31).

   B. Sacrifice and Violence
   1. The Dual Nature of Sacrifice
     The purpose of sacrifice is to get rid of violence
in the community, or where it has not yet erupted, to
prevent violence from occurring (G:17). This is
perhaps somewhat hard to understand because sacrifice
itself resembles criminal violence; inversely we can
say that there is hardly any form of sacrifice that
cannot be described in terms of violence (G:1). It is
precisely for this reason that sacrifice works as an
antidote since violence is avenged in a manner so that
vengeance does not continue. Perhaps we can clarify
it by saying there is a duality, an ambivalence in

sacrifice. The sacrificial act assumes two opposing aspects:

a) A sacred obligation, neglected at grave peril;

b) A sort of criminal activity entailing perils of equal gravity (G:1).

This is true because of the sacred character of the victim. It is criminal to kill the victim because he is sacred, yet the victim is sacred only because he is to be killed (G:1). As Girard explains further:

> Religion invariably strives to subdue violence, to keep it from running wild. Paradoxically, the religious and moral authorities in a community attempt to instill nonviolence, as an active force into daily life and as a mediating force into ritual life, through the application of violence....the sacrificial act appears as both sinful and saintly..." (G:20).

2. The Sacrificial Crisis

Whenever the difference between sacred and profane threatens to vanish, whenever killing has begun without regard to the sacred and profane, the society is threatened and a crisis results. This can only be corrected by a carefully carried out sacrifice that pays close attention to ritual. Girard calls this the sacrificial crisis and, "...means thereby the shattering of the order that is steadily renewed and guaranteed through sacrificial ritual" (S:26).

In order to avert or correct sacrificial crisis, strict attention must be paid to carrying out sacrificial ritual in a way that violence is averted. This includes such matters as choosing a victim that cannot fight back, a victim that at once fills the dual requirement of being close enough to be seen as vengeance for the acts that could create or created the crisis, yet far enough away that the cycle of vengeance is not begun or continued (G:39).

If a crisis has arisen, extra caution needs to be taken, for we must remember that "At the very height of the crisis, violence becomes simultaneously the instrument, object, and all inclusive subject of desire" (G:144). Thus also, "The more critical the situation, the more "precious" the sacrificial victim must be" (G:18). Vengeance is dangerous to the survival of the community; and thus sacrifice, seen as a controlled form of vengeance, becomes a very delicate matter.

3. Sacrifice and Vengeance

Violence is infectious--it needs to go somewhere. It needs to be avenged "...for it is precisely because they detest violence that men make a duty of vengeance" (G:15). But vengeance is an interminable, infinitely repetitive process (G:14-15). The only way to secure the safety of the group is to check this impulse for revenge (G:21). This is possible via the sacrificial process which "furnishes an outlet for those violent impulses that cannot be mastered by self-restraint.... The sacrificial process prevents the spread of violence by keeping vengeance in check" (G:18). It achieves this task through the surrogate victim. "In destroying the surrogate victim, people believe that they are ridding themselves of some present ill. And indeed they are, for they are effectively doing away with those forms of violence that beguile the imagination and provoke emulation" (G:82). Thus the vengeance cycle is broken.

4. Primitive or Sacrificial Vengeance versus Modern or Judicial Vengeance

According to Girard's analysis, primitive societies operate on a basis of private vengeance, whereas modern societies operate on a basis of public vengeance administered by a judicial system (G:15).

> There is no difference of principle between private and public vengeance; but on the social level, the difference is enormous. Under the pyblic (sic) system, an act of vengeance is no longer avenged; the process is terminated, the danger of escalation averted (G:16).

Thus in primitive societies, sacrifice holds private vengeance in check; whereas in modern societies vengeance is carried out by the judicial system (G:18). There is an essential difference between the two:

> In the case of sacrifice, the designated victim does not become the object of vengeance because he is a replacement, is not the "right" victim. In the judicial system the violence does indeed fall on the "right" victim; but it falls with such force, such resounding authority, that no retort is possible (G:22).
> If our own system seems more rational, it is because it conforms more strictly to the principle of vengeance. Its insistence on the punishment of the guilty party underlines this fact (G:22).

Furthermore, instead of trying to sabotage or divert vengeance, our system rationalizes vengeance and its use without fear of contamination (G:22). Girard has much more to say about vengeance as it relates to a sacrificial system and this sub-topic would in itself warrant a more extensive study. In my opinion Girard gives undue praise to our judicial system.

5. Violence Deflected out of the Community via the Surrogate Victim

When the violence and other evils intimately related to violence are loaded upon the surrogate victim and thereby deflected out of the community, three benefits accrue to the community: the community is saved from self-destruction, the community is unified, and life and work within the community become healthy and fruitful.

The first is the most obvious. As the violence is led out of the community by sacrifice, the community is saved from the destructive effects of its own violence. Girard points out that the fact that Cain had no sacrificial outlet, whereas Abel did, resulted in Cain's act of murder (G:4). Jacob and Isaac slaughtered animals to interpose between them. The meat was presented as a meal and Jacob hid inside the animal skins, representing the insulation that prevents contact that would lead to violence (the curse).

The community, subsumed under the single head of the surrogate victim, is once again unified (G:102). The function of sacrifice in fact requires "violent unanimity" (G:101). The surrogate victim is paraded through the community prior to sacrifice and attendance is always compulsory. Everyone needs to take part in the violence of the sacrifice of the surrogate victim. In this way unity is achieved through a common and unified act. Girard correctly points out though that "The best men can hope for in their quest for nonviolence is the unanimity-minus-one of the surrogate victim" (G:259).

The health and productivity of every aspect of the community is dependent on this unity and is a direct result of it. "When people no longer live in harmony with one another, the sun still shines and the rain still falls, to be sure, but the fields are less well tended, the harvests less abundant (G:8). When the spouse is out wreaking vengeance, less time is spent at home and the fertility rate of the community drops as well. Thus Girard sees an essential unity in all

sacrificial rites--they all derive from violence
(G:8).

6.   Sacrifice and Sacrificial Ritual

Key to the whole concept of sacrifice is that it
requires a certain degree of misunderstanding to
achieve its goals. The people carrying out the
sacrifice cannot recognize that it is a process
emanating from within themselves, or they will not
carry it out and the community will be at the mercy of
uncontrolled private vengeance.

> Once we have focused attention on the
> sacrificial, the object originally singled
> out for violence fades from view.
> Sacrificial substitution implies a degree of
> misunderstanding. Its vitality as an
> institution depends on its ability to conceal
> the displacement upon which the rite is
> based. It must never lose sight entirely,
> however, of the original object, or cease to
> be aware of the act of transference from that
> object to the surrogate victim; without that
> awareness no substitution can take place and
> the sacrifice loses all efficacy (G:5).

It is the duty of sacrificial ritual to achieve
this delicate degree of misunderstanding. The awesome
machinery of ritual also hides those properties of
violence that sacrifice has appropriated and that
present possible danger, particularly the ability of
violence to spread from one to another (G:19). Girard
defines ritual as "the imitation and reenactment of
spontaneous, unanimous violence" (G:99). Even though
the orientation--the purpose--of rites are peaceful,
rites are violent in order to abolish violence. "Even
the most violent rites are specifically designed to
abolish violence" (G:103). The "primitive people
themselves recognize this violence (but) in an almost
entirely dehumanized form; that is under the deceptive
guise of the sacred" (G:30). This becomes easier to
understand if we recognize that "people can dispose of
their violence more efficiently if they regard the
process not as something emanating from within
themselves; but as a necessity imposed from without, a
divine decree whose least infraction calls down
terrible punishment" (G:14). That is why, Girard
claims, sacrifice has often been described as an "act
of mediation between a sacrificer and a 'deity'"
(G:6).

7. The Role of Religion in Violence and Sacrifice

Because it is religion's duty to obscure the real reason for sacrifice (people's violent mimetic impulse), when a need to truly understand arises, the explanations of religion become unsatisfactory (G:35). Nevertheless, religion is far from "useless." It takes violence out of human hands and transforms it into a form of violence that can be kept in check by performance of the appropriate rites, thus transcending the vengeance cycle (G:134).

"Religion in its broadest sense, then, must be another term for that obscurity that surrounds human effort to defend itself by curative or preventative means against humanity's own violence" (G:23). Girard further defines religion as "simply another term for the surrogate victim, who reconciles mimetic oppositions and assigns a sacrificial goal to the mimetic impulse" (G:307).

C. Mimetic Rivalry as the Cause of Violence

1. Mimetic Rivalry (Mimetische Struktur der Begierde)

Everyone is taught from the time of birth to imitate an example, and this is done throughout life. However, in imitating another person, one eventually ends up desiring the same thing. At this point the two become rivals and mimetic rivalry is the result. The whole process is called the "mimetic structure of desire." Whenever two people desire the same thing, whenever two superpowers want to own the same piece of land, mimetic rivalry leads to violence. Often the two characters are imitating each other. Freud characterized this in his analysis of sexual desires: a son imitates his father and desires his mother, resulting in a rivalry. Girard extends this to all desires and assigns a mimetic structure to all of society. Violence, he adds, is a direct result of this structure (S:20-27).

2. The Nature of Violence
a) Creates Misunderstanding and Blindness

Anger, the basis of violence is both powerful and blind. It is powerful because decency and goodwill can't withstand it and it is blind because it loses sight of the object of anger (S:17). How can violence then ever be rationalized? The power and blindness of violence, operating together do not create a good mix. Further, "People always find it distasteful to admit that the 'reasons' on both sides of a dispute are equally valid--which is to say that violence operates without reasons" (G:46). That is not to say that

"reasons" aren't given. Violence can marshal some
very convincing "reasons" to justify its existence.

b)   In essence Mimetic, Self-Propogating
Vengeance

In our section on sacrifice and vengeance we dealt
already to some extent with the nature of violence.
We said that violence is infectious, mimetic, and as
such is imitated over and over again. Girard claims
that violence is self-propogating because only
violence can put an end to violence. "Everyone wants
to strike the last blow, and reprisal can thus follow
reprisal without any true conclusion ever being
reached" (G:26). When we try to subdue this rampant
violence, the time comes when it can only be countered
by more violence: "whether we fail or succeed in our
effort to subdue it, the real victor is always
violence itself" (G:31). We remember, of course, that
even sacrifice and judicial vengeance are forms of
violence.

c) Violence seeks a Surrogate Victim (Scapegoat)

Though violence is not to be denied, it can be
diverted to another object, something it can sink its
teeth into (G:4). If violence is left unappeased and
the initial object remains persistently out of reach
while continuing to provoke hostility, violence seeks
and always finds a surrogate victim. "The creature
that excited its fury is abruptly replaced by another,
chosen only because it is vulnerable and close at
hand" (G:2).

d) Sexuality and Violence

Girard sees both sexuality and violence as basic in
the religious life of people. While he sees many
connections between sexuality and violence, he assigns
a more central role to violence. Violence is more
pure and can operate for a variety of reasons,
including sexual, whereas sexual desire "is impure
because it has to do with violence" (G:34). People
can see the anger and violence of others but not their
own, whereas in the sexual, one can see one's own
drive (S:16). Girard concedes that sexual desire
possesses much power, since it "is one of those
primary forces whose sovereignty over humans is
assured by firm belief of humans that they are
sovereign over it" (G:34). Sexual desire often leads
to quarrels, jealous rages and mortal combat and is a
permanent source of disorder even in the most
harmonious of communities (G:35). Girard sees other
connections between sexual desire and violence: both
will attach themselves to surrogate objects if the

original object of desire is unattainable; both if
repressed, accumulate energy that sooner or later
bursts forth, creating havoc; and third, the shift
from sexuality to violence or vice versa are both
easily made, i.e.: "Thwarted sexuality leads naturally
to violence, just as lovers' quarrels often end in an
amorous embrace" (G:35).

Girard raises one additional issue when he asks if
the taboo of menstruation is the half-suppressed
desire to place the blame for all forms of violence on
women (G:36).

D. The Surrogate and Sacrificial Victim (Activation of the Scapegoat Mechanism (Sündenbockmechanismus))

1. Choosing the Victim

For the sake of simplicity I will list some of the
criteria of a sacrificial victim, as Girard gives
them, in point form.

a) The victim is chosen because he/she/it is
vulnerable and close at hand (G:2).

b) The more critical the situation, the more
"precious the victim must be" (G:18).

c) Whether the victims were actual or figurative,
animate or inanimate, they are always incapable of
propogating further vengeance (G:18).

d) The victim cannot be defined in terms of
innocence or guilt. "There is no question of
'expiation.'" Rather, society is seeking to deflect
upon a relatively indifferent victim, a "sacrificible"
victim, the violence that would otherwise be vented on
its own members, the people it most desires to protect
(G:4).

e) The sacrificial process requires "a complete
separation of the sacrificed victim from those beings
for whom the victim is a substitute but also...a
similarity between both parties" (G:39). This has
been called a crisis of distinctions. Both too much
similarity or too much differentiation can send the
whole process into confusion.

i) Similarities: All victims, whether human or
animal, must bear a certain resemblance to the
object(s) they replace in order to be suitable for
sacrifice; they must bear a sharp resemblance to the
human categories excluded from the ranks of the
"sacrificable" otherwise the violent impulse would
remain unsatisfied. This resemblance must not be
carried to the extreme of assimilation but rather

maintain a degree of difference that forbids all
possible disastrous confusion (G:11,12).

   ii) Differences: All sacrificial victims, "are
invariably distinguishable from the non-sacrificable
beings by one essential characteristic: between these
victims and the community a crucial social link is
missing" (G:13). They are "exterior or marginal
individuals, incapable of establishing or sharing the
social bonds that link the rest of the inhabitants.
Their status as foreigners, or enemies, their servile
condition, or simply their age prevents these victims
from fully integrating themselves into the community"
(G:12). Thus, "they can be exposed to violence
without fear of reprisal. Their death does not
automatically entail an act of vengeance" (G:13).

   2. The Double Substitution
   Girard insists that on a few occasions there are
two victims. The first is the surrogate victim who
comes from within and substitutes for the community,
and the second, the sacrificial victim, takes the
place of the first and by necessity comes from outside
the community. The second, which is the only true
"ritualistic" substitution is superimposed on the
first as the substitution of a victim for the
surrogate victim (G:102,269). This is difficult to
comprehend because Girard usually speaks only of one
victim using either designation interchangeably.
Schwager too speaks only of one substitution except in
his analysis of Girard's thought where he briefly
mentions that Girard mentions two substitutions. For
the understanding of the theories of both Girard and
Schwager it is not necessary that we consider two
substitutions.

   3. The Dual Nature of the Victim: Sacred and
Profane
   "The scapegoat mechanism achieves the fundamental
difference between profane and sacred, between human
and nonhuman" (G:40). Seen at once as too sacred to
be killed (yet only because he/she/it is to be killed)
and as the epitome of evil, the victim brings about
the formal identification of violence with the sacred.
The community alternately worships and despises the
victim. They despise the victim because it represents
all that is evil. On the other hand the victim is
worshipped and honored because it causes all good in
the community to happen by carrying away the
dissension, and all other evil caused by violence. We
mentioned earlier how the victim draws to itself all
tensions, feuds, rivalries--all the violence of the

community--and transforms baneful violence into beneficial violence, into harmony and abundance (G:7,95).

How else can we explain it? The victim carries all evil and thus causes all good? The victim represents all evil and thus represents all good? The victim absorbs all violence and thus portrays the sacred? Are violence and the sacred one and the same? Girard says, "Religion shelters us from violence just as violence seeks shelter in religion" (G:24).

E. <u>Summary and Remarks</u>

Schwager summarizes Girard's thinking along five points:

1. The fundamental human desire is in and of itself not directed towards a specific object. It strives after that which has been shown by another desire to be worth striving for. It imitates an example.

2. Through the mimesis of a foreign (exemplary) striving, a conflict arises, because the second desire strives for the same object as the first. Thus the example becomes at the same time a rival. Meanwhile the fought over object is lost sight of.... The rivalry eventually tends towards violence, which by itself now seems worth striving for. It becomes a sign of a successful life worth striving for.

3. Since all people tend towards violence, a peaceful co-existence is in no way to be taken for granted. Decency and good will (social contract) do not suffice. Erupting rivalries can easily endanger the existing order.... New dimensions of relative peace can arise, however, where the reciprocating aggressions suddenly are upset into a unified violence of all against one (scapegoat mechanism).

4. Through the collective loading of the passions upon the scapegoat, he is at the same time made sacred. He appears both as accursed and a bringer of salvation. A sacred threat emanates from him. New taboos and a new social order arise around him.

5. In the sacrifices the original collective transfer of violence onto the arbitrary scapegoat is carried out in a context of strongly controlled ritual. The internal aggressions are thereby once more led to the outside, and the community is saved from self-destruction (S:57).

A few questions and applicatory comments:

1. Do sports such as football and hockey constitute ritualized violence in our society? Do

they fit into Girard's thesis of deflecting violence
out of the community into religious ritual?

2.   Does the hired pastor in our church system fit
into Girard's analysis as to a choice of victim?
(section D,1.e). Does the pastor's similarity yet
difference (in coming from the outside) cause him/her
to qualify as "sacrificable" and become the scapegoat
when trouble arises?

3.   What about the nuclear situation? Girard says
we are trying to multiply our victims in a desperate
attempt to secure ourselves from violence. "When men
believe they can actually feel the breath of a Homeric
Cyclops at their backs, they are apt to resort to all
means at their disposal, to embrace all possible
precaution. It seems safer to over react than to
under react" (G:33).

In speaking about nuclear weapons and nuclear
violence Schwager quotes Girard from a discussion:

> The specialists tell us, without batting an
> eyelash, that only this violence protects us.
> It won't take long anymore, until we will
> understand, why people throw their own
> children in the fiery furnace of the idol
> Moloch and thereby could believe in this
> manner to be protecting themselves against a
> worse violence" (S:42).

III.   Do We Need a Scapegoat? Schwager's Application of
       Girard's Thesis to the Bible

A.   Old Testament: From the God of Vengeance to
the God of Peace
1. Violence among People
Schwager sees violence epitomized as the sin of
sins in the Old Testament. Violence is the sum total
of all sin. All other sin can be seen and described
from that context for every sin against a fellow human
tends towards violence (S:59).

He begins by explaining that there are over 600
instances in which the Old Testament talks about
kings, individuals, and groups of people destroying
and killing each other. In addition the flood
narrative is decisive, for it summarizes all sin by
the word violence (hamas). "Now the earth was
corrupt in God's sight, and the earth was filled with
violence" (Gen 6:11; cf 6:13).

That same designation of all sin as "violence"
(hamas) is also used in Ezekiel 7:11 and Jonah 3:8.
The summary of a list of sins is often given as

violence or bloodshed: "bloodshed follows bloodshed"
(Hos 4:2) or "they multiply lies and violence" (Hos
12:1-2). In Micah's discourses on evil (Mic 1:2-3:12;
6:1-7:7) evil is summarized as "all lie in wait for
blood" (7:2). In explaining Israel's unfaithfulness
from the beginning, Ezekiel accuses the people of
being "full of blood-guilt" due to their shedding of
blood, which he mentions six times (16:1-63; 23:1-49;
22:1-27). Violence is seen as the scepter of the
godless and the essence of godlessness (Ezek 7:11).
Isaiah accuses the people of having their "hands
defiled by blood," "deeds of violence are in their
hands" and "they make haste to shed innocent blood"
(59:2-7). The evil deeds people commit are all of
violence. They don't do anything else. That is why
they are quick to shed blood" (S:61).

The expressions about violence universalize in two
ways. "On the one hand all interpersonal offences are
included in this understanding. On the other hand no
person is excluded from violent striving" (S:63).

2. The Violent Yahweh

Many texts lend credence to the view that Israel
understood the might and power of their God especially
in terms of Yahweh's bloodshedding and violence. God
is seen as Warrior-God from the earliest times of
their existence. During the time of the prophets God
is often seen as an angry judge who reacts vehemently
to sin and whose blood thirstiness at times leads to
the interpretation that God takes joy in killing (Ezek
21:13-20) and/or kills indiscriminately (Ezek 21:8f.,
cf. Jer 25:32f.). "The universality of human violence
corresponds to the universality of the avenging and
judgmental divine violence" (cf. Jer 49:20ff) (S:65).
There are approximately one thousand instances in the
Old Testament where it is said that the wrath of God
burns: God punishes with death and ruin; God judges
like a devouring fire; God takes vengeance and
threatens destruction; God manifests power and glory
in war; and God holds judgment as an angry avenger.
No other theme appears as often as that of the bloody
deeds of God (S:65-66).

Schwager claims that the overwhelming majority of
the Old Testament texts about the wrath of God can be
classified into four categories (S:66-72):

1. God appears as an irrational Being that kills
or desires to kill without understandable reason.

2. God reacts towards the previous evil deeds of
people, and carries out the vengeance himself.

3. God punishes the evildoer, in anger handing them over to other (cruel) people.

4. The evildoers punish themselves, in that their deeds fall back upon their own heads (S:72).

Let me briefly explain the four categories before we analyze them. The first category, referring to irrational reaction is represented by such examples as Usa reaching out to help balance the falling Ark of the Covenant and thus is struck down by God (2 Sam 6:6) or the threat of God to kill Moses for apparently no reason at all (Exod 4:24). The second category implies that following the covenant is a matter of life and death and is represented by passages such as Lev 26:3ff and Deut 30:19. The third category, where people are seen as executors of God's violence, in that God uses other people to carry out his wrath, is very common. One reads often of how God commands Israel to kill certain people because of their sin (in over one hundred verses God directly commands that people be killed) or to destroy other nations because of the same. This often worked against Israel as well, in that Israel is punished by God through other nations (Ezek 21:31, Ps 44:11, Isa 19:2, Jer 51:20ff). The fourth category, of which there are over seventy occurrences, are passages or instances where God is not directly visible. The idea of punishment is still there but the evil deeds backlash upon the people who perpetrate them (Isa 50:11; Jer 44:8; Ps 7:13-17; Prov 8:36, 26:27).

Category 1 is very seldom used and Schwager therefore concludes that passages of this type can be discounted in our attempt to understand the relationship between Yahweh and violence. The differences between categories 2 and 3 are more verbal than realistic and one therefore cannot make a distinction between the two. This is clearly indicated by such texts as Ezekiel 21:31 and Jeremiah 22:25f. which combine both motives, thereby emphasizing that the two are one and the same. Direct intervention by God such as slaying the firstborn of Egypt (Exod 12:29) or the earth swallowing up Korah, Dathan, Abiram in the desert (Num 16:29-32) happens relatively seldom. "Seen from the perspective of experience, the concern is always over human violence which becomes interpreted as acts of God. Whether the texts speak of a direct or indirect working of Yahweh makes no relevant difference" (S:73).

Are we confronted with a new form of violence when we consider category 4? Schwager insists that

ultimately we are not. A synthesis is suggested in
Isaiah 50:11. "Practically in all instances in the
Old Testament where one or another form of
self-punishment is spoken of, it can be shown to be
also the fulfillment of the divine wrath" (S:76).
Conversely, "wherever the divine wrath and the divine
vengeance are spoken about, concrete acts among people
are meant, by which the perpetrators of violence
mutually punish themselves" (S:76). According to
Girard's thesis, wherever a sacred violence is spoken
of, people are fighting with each other. This is
evident in the Old Testament where God is seen as a
devouring fire and as a wrathful and vengeful God. At
the same time it becomes clear that people excite this
anger and that they also carry out the violent deeds.
Progressively the Old Testament realizes that the
violence of God is the people's own violence ascribed
to God.

Concerning Yahweh's conduct towards human deeds,
the Old Testament does not answer in singular fashion.
There are two unclarified parallel strands. According
to the one, God is excited by the human evil and in
anger eggs the people on (Isa 19:2; cf. 13:17). These
kinds of texts ascribe to God a very active role. In
the second strand the punishing and avenging deeds of
God consist only in hiding/covering his face. When
God leaves people to their own devices, they begin to
destroy one another (Isa 64:5f) and when he hides his
face from them, nothing good ensues and they go down
to destruction (Ps 81:12f; Ps 143:7). Only where the
face of God shines can people truly live. The
narratives of the Fall and of Cain and Abel help us
clarify the relationship between the two strands.

When Adam and Eve sin, they hide from God. When
they are sent out of the Garden, they are sent away
from the presence of God, and God covers his face
before them. The worst consequence is the Cain and
Abel story. Now that people have been sent out of the
presence of God, everyone can expect to be killed by
another, even by his or her own sibling. Abel's death
can be seen as the paradigm of human dying because it
was the first. God's earlier warning that death is
the result of sin is fulfilled in that when Adam and
Eve sin, God's presence is withdrawn from them; then
the first-born, Cain, kills Abel, the second-born, his
brother. Now Cain finds that he must hide from God's
face as well and is afraid that he will be killed as a
result (Gen 4:14).

The narratives of the Fall and Cain and Abel
make it clear that the last reason for God's
concealing himself lies in the fact, that the
sinful and violent people have to hide
themselves spontaneously before God.
Although God does not directly kill the
guilty people, his warning comes true. The
people have made it come true themselves, in
that one murdered the other and the murderer
has to count on the fact, to be himself
killed as well (S:79-80).

Then the Lord instituted the principle of vengeance
in order to keep killing within bounds and subvert it
as much as possible. Thus anyone who kills Cain will
receive seven-fold vengeance. But even this was a
two-edged sword, for when Lamech, Cain's fifth
descendant, came along, he said that he would avenge
seventy-seven times (Gen 4:23f). Instead of vengeance
serving as antidote against violence, it tends towards
the opposite. That is why we read that during the
time of Noah "the earth was corrupt in God's sight,
and the earth was filled with violence" (Gen 6:11).

We can conclude then that the relationship of God
to violence is a singular one, Schwager says. Though
God threatens sinful people with death, God's own self
does not become violent. God just sends away the
guilty. In a world where God's face does not shine,
work and childbearing become difficult and people tend
to murder each other.

Not all Old Testament passages fit this mold, but
the theory of Girard that violence ascribed to the
sacred is actually the people's own violence
misunderstood, throws a new light onto the central
theme of the Old Testament.

   3. Rivalries and Jealousy

Girard says that violence arises out of the
mimesis. People don't in and of themselves desire the
same object but rather an "example" has shown them
that it is worth striving for. The two end up
striving for the same thing, thus causing jealousy.
Since the rival remains the example (model) even the
jealous feelings are imitated. The working of the
mimesis causes the rivalry to keep rising until it
ends in violence.

Schwager sees this theme as prominent in the Old
Testament. Jealousy and rivalry developed between
Cain and Abel; between the shepherds of Abraham and
those of Lot; between Sarah and Hagar; between the
wives of Jacob, Esau, and Jacob; between Joseph and

his brothers; Miriam and Aaron against Moses; Korah,
Dathan, and Abiram against Moses; between David and
Saul; between the sons of David; between Israel
(Ephraim) and Judah, and so on.

Even God is portrayed as a rival and as a jealous
God. In the account of Eve and the snake, God is seen
as a rival of Eve--knowing good and evil, whereas Eve
does not. Yahweh is seen as a rival of other gods and
stimulates Israel to jealousy (Deut 32:31). Sometimes
Yahweh insists on jealousy, inspiring Israel to
believe in a monotheism in faith and practice, as in
Deutero-Isaiah. Here it first became visible that God
is no rival to other gods because they do not exist
(S:85).

4. The Mimesis

If violence follows jealousy and rivalry which
arise out of the mimesis, the imitation of foreign
models, who or what are the models in the Old
Testament? Schwager says that the key to this theme
is found in Israel's imitation of other nations.
Again and again Israel turns to worship the idols of
the other nations (Deut 8:19; 11:28; Judg 2:12; 2:19;
Jer 2:8), desiring always to imitate them. Israel
desires their possessions (Jer 2:23f), their horses
and riders (Ezek 23:5f), and their kings (1 Sam
8:5-9;19f). This mimesis, this running after other
gods, other nations, imitating their violence and
making military covenants with them causes Israel's
sin to fall back on their heads. It is the horses and
riders Israel desired that end up fulfilling the wrath
of God upon Israel. Here we see the connection
between the mimesis and the punishing violence.

5. The Projection of Sacred Conceptions

Girard holds that by the attachment of all violent
conceptions onto a scapegoat--a sacrifice--the
sacrifice is made sacred because it comes as a
peacemaker to a threatened community. Israel had a
developed sacrificial ritual. But the Old Testament
also contains a massive critique of sacrifice--that of
other nations and also especially of Israel. In brief
we can say that what God wants from Israel is not
sacrifice, not the blood of animals, but love and the
knowledge of God (Amos 5:21-25; Mic 6:6f; Jer 7:21f;
Ps 40:7f). It reminds one of a child asking, "Mom,
what do you want for Christmas?" and the mother
answers, "All I want is obedient children." Whereas
that seems good enough for the parent--and good enough
for God--the Israelites, like children, want to make a
sacrifice. God even rejects sacrifices because the

people's hands are full of blood (Isa 1:11-15; Jer 19:3-6). God wants people to abandon bloodshed of all forms, rather than using one form to control the other. The prophets tell the Israelites that due to the nature of their sacrifices, they don't cover or protect them from their guilt but only serve to increase it (S:100).

6. The Band of Perpetrators of Violence (Gewalttäter)

In the theory of Girard, the transfer of violence from the community to the scapegoat is a collective act. In order to see if this is present in the Old Testament one cannot look to the testimony of those who participate in the transferring process, for they need to be blind to their involvement in order to do it. One needs to find a person who, surrounded and persecuted by the majority, is the scapegoat and gives an alternative perspective. We have an example of this in the Old Testament, presented primarily in the Psalms and some of the prophets. Approximately one hundred of one hundred fifty Psalms speak of enemies. The number one problem is that these enemies are out to destroy the persecuted one--Israel, Jerusalem, the Psalmist. God, the lamenting one, and the enemies all are at times the cause of the lament, including being forsaken by God.

Psalm 69 is a prime example of the enemies theme. The three points given are: 1) the enemies are very numerous, 2) they are mendacious, and 3) they hate without reason (S:108). All enemies are united against the one Israel as they project their own evil and fear upon that one. God gives a promise, however, to take the rejected stone and make it into the cornerstone. Jerusalem will become the cornerstone for all people (S:116).

7. The Revelation of the True God and the Overcoming of Violence

a) The Working of God Through the Word

The God of Israel is not a God who manifests himself by evidence of might but rather through promises, demands, and threats that are fulfilled in the course of time. Thus what Israel owes Yahweh are not sacrifices, but rather trust, faith and obedience. God freed Israel from foreign Lordship, not so that Israel could be their own Lord but in order to be Lord over Israel. Though humans always imitate someone, they are now no longer to imitate other nations but to serve God and obey God's word (S:120).

Since falsehood, violence, and alliances with foreign powers were Israel's worst sins against Yahweh (Hos 12:1 etc.) and chariots were the beginning of sin in Jerusalem (Mic 1:13-cf. 5:9), true faith is a matter of choosing between violence (military defense) and Yahweh (cf. Isa 2:4). Yahweh calls for total rejection of violence--a choice between life and death (Jer 21:8f).

b) The New Collective (Community)

The Old Testament is witness to a belief that does not need a scapegoat in order for peace to be achieved. Rather than all converging upon a sacrifice, God stands by the rejected one with a helpful and merciful word. But how does a new community arise in order to establish a kingdom of peace?

Schwager says that God's word needs to be revealed to people in order for them to see their own violence. The revelation is thereby identical with the overcoming of violence among people. The people need to be taught the word that has more power to save them than their violence. "Peace becomes possible because instruction comes out of Zion, and the word of God out of Jerusalem. The word of instruction achieves the new community" (S:128).

c) The Spirit of God and Love among People

The gathering of the new community is the work of Yahweh. The people's part is to have their hearts converted. The promised kingdom of peace includes people turning away from violence and seeking unity. This is possible because they will be taught directly by God writing it into their hearts. According to Girard, people tend towards a mimesis; this will happen as long as people need examples (models), for the imitation of teachers leads to rivalries. The tendency to violence can only be broken when people no longer need to teach each other but when people find their striving in the Spirit of God.

8. The Suffering Servant

In his analysis of Isaiah 40-55, Schwager states that whether it is all the nations against Israel or all evil-doers against a righteous one is immaterial to our discussion and the questions we want to answer.

God teaches his servant by his word every day--"He opens his ear every day." The result is that God's servants do not react to the violence of their enemies with vengeance. Instead of destroying enemies, they become a light to all nations. People thought that the servant was suffering on his own account, but had to realize that it was because of their sin. We recall the discussion earlier of the belief that violence (sin) fell back upon the heads of the perpetrators.

The crucial verse for Schwager is Isaiah 53:6b. This is also the crucial verse insofar as Girard's theory is concerned. The text reads: "and the Lord has laid on him the iniquity of us all." Or as the German reads "But the Lord threw all our sins upon him." This translation makes us think that God acted in a juridical sense. Schwager suggests another translation: "But the Lord permitted it, that we threw all our sins upon him" (S:139). He claims the synthetic Hebrew Language makes no real difference between an active causing and a passive permitting. Thus the two translations can be said to mean essentially the same thing, whether it is Yahweh's violent deed or whether Yahweh permits him to be turned into the hands of violent people. It is essential to Girard's theory that the people project their own violence upon the scapegoat.

Schwager concludes that because the suffering servant held his back and cheeks out for torture, the sins of the perpetrators could not fall back upon them and they could come to a better insight.

B.   New Testament: Jesus as Scapegoat of the World

   1.   The Hermeneutical Question

Girard and Schwager see the key to the understanding of the New Testament, including its relation to the Old Testament in the verse: "The stone which the builders rejected, has become the cornerstone." In this key verse one has the summary of the early Christian kerygma. The hermeneutic key within the verse is that through the rejection of the Son, the hidden truth becomes visible. "The collective blindness assists the revelation" (S:148). Together with this verse comes the parable of the wicked tenants of the vineyard (Mark 12:1-10 and parallels). The three points of the parable are: 1) Jesus' claim to be the beloved Son, 2) his own separation from the violent oppressors and 3) the positioning of his coming within the dealings of God with a stiff-necked people. In addition the parable points out mimetic material greed as the cause of the murder.

   2.   The Underlying Will to Kill and Lie
   a)   The Announcement of the Destruction of the Temple

The destruction of the Temple, the visible center of Israel, and the end time wars demonstrate the underlying violence that is present in Israel, and which is ascribed to the whole human race.

b) <u>The Woes against the Teachers of the Law and Pharisees</u>

While the Teachers of the Law and Pharisees recognize the sin and bloodiness of their ancestors in killing the prophets, they don't count themselves within the same tradition. Jesus accuses them of being full of lies and violence and warns them that they are standing in the same tradition as their forefathers. The warning causes them all the more not to see it, since they reject it. Their failure to recognize that they could be doing the same as their forefathers causes them to do the same.

c) <u>The Separation of People on account of Jesus</u>

Jesus' coming brings a sword, a fact of his ministry. The sword is not wielded by Jesus but rather comes as a result of his coming. He opens interpersonal relations and lays them bare; the sword is the result. Even the announcement of Jesus' coming caused Herod to have the babies killed, for he was anticipating a rivalry.

d) <u>The Murderer from the Beginning</u>

In John 8:39-44 Jesus tells the Jews that they are not truly children of Abraham or they would not try to kill him who brought them the truth from God. Rather, they are possessed by the same spirit as Cain was, by the murderer from the beginning; the devil himself is their father. In this murderer is no truth at all. The key to change for the Jews is recognition but they cannot recognize him because they are full of hate. Ultimately it was the hate of the world that killed Jesus, for it was through the Jews that the hate of the world came upon him. Thus through Jesus the total exposing of Israel and the world took place. 1 John 3:11ff explains that hatred was the cause of Jesus' death. "It follows therefore that not only does every murderer hate, but conversely, everyone who hates is a murderer" (S:168).

e) <u>No Difference between Jews and Gentiles</u>

Schwager asserts that Paul's thought stands fully in line with that of Jesus and the Gospels. He makes the same two accusations of lies and violence that Jesus made to his opponents. Paul also understood sin as bringing death to the world—not just spiritual death but a violent physical death (Rom 3:10-18; Rom 5:12; 6:23). Sin effected death in his life (Rom

7:10,13), for he points out his own involvement in
trying to destroy Christians (Gal 1:13). Paul also
insists that eagerness for the letter of the law leads
sooner or later to death, even to a physical death (2
Cor 3:6). This is supported in John 19:7 where the
Jews cry to Pilate, "We have a law, and according to
that law he must die" (S:170-171).

   3. The Kingdom of God and the beginning of the
New Community

   a) God's Work and Human Work

   If the word of revelation exposes the underlying
passions, the scapegoat mechanism loses its
effectiveness. The exposure of people's underlying
desire to kill causes people to decide either to
destroy each other or to await proper understanding
from a new source. Jesus preached that this new peace
does not come about by human effort but by the kingdom
of God which is achieved without human contribution;
it is a gift of God. This does not mean that people
can watch God set up the kingdom but rather that God's
actions call people into a new responsibility. God's
actions desire to _enable_ people to new actions of
their own. Thus we can say also that healing--and
other ethical dimensions of the Gospel--and the
kingdom of God go hand in hand. God's word is not an
empty word, for it achieves what it promises, as
Matthew points out by reporting twenty-five cases of
healing. Along the same line we can also say that God
needs people, for Jesus works through and heals people
who have faith. He does not deal with lifeless
objects.

   b) Not Resisting Evil

   The New Testament never separates inner and outer
response. Thus the command to love enemies and never
to return evil with evil belong to the central
structure of the New Testament message (Mt 5:39; Luke
6:27ff; Rom 12:17-21; 1 Peter 3:9; 1 Thess 5:15).
Schwager goes on to call Lk 6:27ff the Magna Carta of
Christian Ethics (S:179). As a result of the mimesis,
violence is a highly communicable disease. If we
attempt to confront evil violence head on, we will
fall victim to it. To love enemies, and return evil
with good represents the only way to break through the
vicious (Devil's) circle of the mimesis and of
violence (S:178). Further, the command in Matthew
18:22 to forgive seventy-seven times is a reversal of
Genesis 4:23 where Lamech vows to avenge seventy-seven
times.

The lordship of violence can only then be
inwardly broken, if the point never arrives,
at which forgiving love capitulates before it
and begins itself to imitate evil through a
corresponding reciprocation (S:181).

   c) Mimesis and Discipleship (Nachfolge)
Schwager draws a distinction between Nachahmung
(imitation) and Nachfolge (following after,
discipleship). Imitation even in love always ends in
violence, and a strict imitation in a different
situation causes the imitator to do something that
totally contradicts his/her model. The call of Jesus
is neither imitation (mimesis) nor spontaneity, but
rather following after discipleship.

   Imitation leads to sacrificial offerings which
Jesus says God does not want (Matt 12:1-8; Luke
6:1-5). God wants the well-being of creation, not
offering (Matt 5:23f). This is shown further by the
healings on the Sabbath: no antithesis exists between
service of God and the well-being of people.

   Though we should have and want to have the same
closeness to God that Jesus has, there is no rivalry,
because Jesus calls us his friends (John 15:15). He
tells us everything the Father told him (John 15:15)
and prays that his followers may be united to him
(John 17:20f; 14:20). David and Jonathan had no
rivalry because they loved each other like their own
life. Jesus loved his disciples more than his own
life (John 15:13). Before disciples become friends,
however, they need to die to their own self-serving
striving.

   d) Jesus' Attempt at a New Community
Though Jesus through his life and death made it
possible for everyone to join the new way by
discipleship, it happened only with a few. But Jesus
didn't call people to discipleship just for their own
salvation, but rather to make them fishers of men
(Mark 1:16-20). The blindness which caused the
(corner) stone to be rejected and thus becomes the
central hermeneutical question also caused the goal of
a new community not to be fully realized while Jesus
was on earth.

   4. All Against One: Jesus as Scapegoat
Everyone unites together to kill him: Pharisees,
Sadducees, Zealots, Essenes, highpriests and teachers
of the Law. The whole Sanhedrin decides (Mark
15:1); all the highpriests and elders made a united
decision to have him killed (Matt 27:1); the whole
gathering (community) (Luke 23:1), i.e., large crowds

(same word for crowds used as to designate those that
followed him around countryside) participates; and
even enemies such as Herod and Pilate become united as
friends.   Jesus was left completely alone; even his
own disciples left him.   Thus they also were caused to
stand against him.   Jesus experiences all the enemies
against him, as described in the Old Testament so
vividly, and could be more accurately described as a
persecuted servant than a suffering servant.
Everyone takes part in this persecution, since central
New Testament texts expose an underlying tendency to
falsehood and violence in all people and since in one
form or another the same spirit is active in all
people.   Thus all people secretly stand against Jesus.
The two points we have made are also given in Acts
4:24-27:   1) The enemies don't deal singly, but have
united against Jesus; and 2) the enemies' alliance has
a universal dimension which includes Herod and
Pilate together with the Gentiles and the tribes of
Israel (S:194).   Thus, "all people on earth unite
against Jesus, God's anointed one.   All perpetrators
of violence stand against the holy one" (S:195).
    5. The Son of God as "Necessary" Scapegoat
    Girard says that in the choice of a scapegoat
he/she/it is never more or less guilty than anyone
else.   The case is different with Jesus.   The holy
servant had to suffer, and he had to take the divisive
violence upon himself.   The proclamation of Jesus was
about God's love and in the process he claimed to be
the son of God, calling God his Father (John 15:16ff;
John 8:18ff).   This becomes the key accusation
against Jesus.   People hated Jesus because inwardly
people hate God because God goes against their natural
tendencies.   They need to be transformed by God.   We
must add that the Pharisees weren't normal murderers.
They had a highly developed law.   But because Jesus
put himself above their law, making himself equal with
God, it awakened a basic spirit that is present in all
people.   The people rejecting Jesus are so blinded and
deluded that they can't deal in any other manner.   The
scapegoat couldn't be anyone.   It had to be Jesus
because as the Son of God he exposed their own violent
tendencies by absorbing and taking the people's sin
upon himself.   He thus can reveal to them God's way of
truth and love.   Jesus, as the revelation of God,
becomes the cornerstone.
    6. One for All: The Redemption (Salvation)
    Hebrews 9-13 explains to us the differences and
similarities between OT and NT atonement.   In the

process it uses the word blood 17 times, explaining to
us that in the OT foreign blood (animals) is used, but
in the NT "own" blood refers to the blood of Jesus.
The connection to Melchizedek, however, comes not in
the matter of ritual offering but in the matter of
peace and righteousness.

Christ became sin not in that he had sin but in
that our sin was upon him. The Substitution Theory
becomes inadequate because it just says that Jesus
took the punishment but doesn't emphasize that he took
our sin upon himself as the NT teaches. God forgives
without demanding satisfaction or something in
return--in the same way that Jesus commands his
followers to forgive; only God forgives even more
readily (Luke 15:11-32; Matt 18:23-35). Thus
reconciliation according to 2 Cor 5:19 is God's
refusal to count people's sins against them.

> Salvation is necessary in order that people
> are freed and saved from their inability to
> desire the good. God doesn't demand
> satisfaction but a person must be hauled out
> of his prison, in order that he becomes
> capable of accepting the anticipated love of
> God. Paul therefore turns entreatingly to
> the church: "Let yourselves be reconciled to
> God" (2 Cor 5:20). Not that God has to be
> softened, but that people need to be saved
> from their hate (S:213).

Jesus could die for all because all had united
against him. All banded together against him and
through the crucifixion all could transfer their
grudge against God and their will to kill upon him.

In regular sacrifices a reversal of violence is
effected as sacrifice puts a sacred fear into the
sacrificers. The victims usually responded with
resistance and curses. Jesus, however, responded with
love and forgiveness (Luke 23:24; 1 Pet 2:23). He
didn't despair but left it to the one who judges
righteously. The evidence is his quote of the first
lines of Psalm 22: "My God, My God, why have you
forsaken me?" It is common practice among the Jews to
quote just the first few lines of a Psalm and thereby
mean to be understood to have quoted the whole Psalm.
Schwager insists that this is precisely what Jesus
does. Later in the Psalm the servant is declared
righteous. "The cast out one becomes the true
cornerstone in that he doesn't tend towards vengeance,
but precisely rather saves the people through his
death" (S:218).

7. The Wrath of God

Concerning the wrath of God in the NT, Schwager
deals primarily with Romans 1:18-32. The OT
categories of God's wrath, where he steps in with
violent power or gets others to do the punishing for
him, are not present in Paul. The wrath, according to
Paul, consists in God handing people over to their own
desires, passions, and twisted thinking. People
suffer the result of their own sin, similar to the
narrative of the Fall in Genesis. The unforgiveable
sin and hell consist of people rejecting and resisting
the forgiving and redeeming love of God. They suffer
the disastrous consequences of their own sin. Thus
hell is the total result and the sum total of people's
own sin and the consequence (S: 220-221).

Regarding the judgment and apocalyptic wrath of
God, Schwager says that in the gospels only the
consequences of people's own sin is mentioned. It
never talks of God committing an act of violence.
Thus, he concludes that the true nature of the
apocalyptic wrath is still hidden with God
(S:221-222).

8. The New Community: The Holy Spirit and the
New People of God

The new community begins with the pouring out of
the Holy Spirit. The Holy Spirit, explains Schwager,
is the principle of unity. It is a different peace
and unity than one that comes about by Girard's
scapegoat mechanism. Rather than effecting a unity of
all against one, the Holy Spirit causes people to be
united for one, namely the Lord. Whereas Jesus
effected a unity out of the negative, the Holy Spirit
effected a positive unity.

The Holy Spirit works through the Word--the Living
Word which is Christ. This Word is untainted by
violence. The Holy Spirit working that Word in people
makes it possible for them to totally dedicate
themselves to the cause of Christ.

God is also revealed through God's people. This is
shown in the Magnificat. The mighty lose their throne
and the lowly are lifted up! The lowly can only
remain there if they are servants on the same level as
everyone else. Thus there is no more rivalry.

C. Remarks

Schwager concludes his book by delving into the
issue of Christians persecuting Jews. He insists that
when Christians persecute Jews, they make the
identical mistake that the Pharisees made in

persecuting Jesus. To say that the Jews killed Jesus
is identical to the response of the Pharisees when
they were confronted with their own murderous
inclinations.

Schwager's approach might raise some questions. I
balk at taking theories developed in different
contexts and fields of study and applying them to the
Bible. However I also came to recognize that both
Girard's theory and the Bible arise out of the
interrelation between people and their cultural
contexts. Nevertheless, I feel more comfortable doing
biblical study and applying it outward.

III. Applying Girard and Schwager to Peace Church Understandings

The first positive application we can make is to
begin to see the rootedness of all evil in violence.
As Anabaptists we have tended to isolate violence into
its more visible forms. At that point violence has
already reached a somewhat more advanced stage. It is
also more difficult to combat violence at that stage
because it has become all the more deluded. We need
to, and I think we are beginning to, see violence at
the root of so many of our activities and lifestyles.
Perhaps, as Schwager says, by exposing it, it can be
overcome.

The idea of the mimesis still poses questions for
me. I can see and understand how undue competition
and rivalry can be the result of memesis, but we need
to ask some questions about the competitiveness of
society. Where can we begin to root out unnecessary
rivalry? The concept of rivalries is embedded very
strongly in our society and is not much less frequent
in our churches.

I also question Girard and Schwager in holding that
we are no longer to have models (examples). When we
become disciples of Jesus, Schwager adds, we need no
other teachers. Schwager teaches at the University of
Innsbruck, and surely some students see him as an
example--a model. This concept of models--good
models--has been emphasized very strongly in our
churches, especially for children and youth. One
example is the mentoring program. I believe these
kinds of programs have considerable value.

Another positive aspect we can learn from Schwager
is his insight of a God of Peace in the OT. This was
first introduced to me by Millard Lind's Yahweh is
Warrior and Schwager's study added much to my

understanding of God and war in the OT. As a peace
church we need to continue to do more study of the OT
and war.

Schwager does exclude some key OT passages. While
he would stand by Lind's rejection of synergism, he
doesn't deal with the "absolute miracle" passages to
any real extent. He does hint that he considers them
older exceptions and thus not of much value in
understanding God in the OT. Schwager leans heavily
on the prophets, whereas Lind deals with the
Deuteronomic Writings. Perhaps the two could be
combined.

Another insight that has not received much
attention from Anabaptists is Jesus as scapegoat of
our violence. This definitely is worth more study.

Schwager suggests that not resisting evil with evil
means a more passive stance. He says that dealing
with violence by meeting it head on causes us to fall
into the same trap. What does that say about recent
Mennonite shifts towards more active forms of
nonviolent resistance? My own tendencies are towards
non-violent resistance over against a passive stance.

Book Analysis

Norbert Lohfink (ed.), <u>Gewalt und Gewaltlosigkeit im Alten Testament</u>(CeD 96; Freiberg/Basel/Wien: Herder, 1983). Pp. 256.

by Millard C. Lind

Introduction

This book is another evidence of the growing interest of the ecumenical church in the question of war and violence. It is made up of four essays read at a Catholic Conference, "Arbeitsgemeinschaft deutschsprachiger katholischer Alttestamentlicher," August 24-28, 1981 in Neustift bei Brixon.

The essays read at the conference were:

1. "'Gewalt' als Thema alttestamentlicher Forschung," Lohfink

2. "Die Schichten des Pentateuch und der Krieg," Lohfink

3. "Klagelieder in Israel und Babylonien-verschiedene Deutungen der Gewalt," Lothar Ruppert

4. "Die Botschaft von Gottesknecht--ein Weg zur Uberwindung der Gewalt," Ernst Haag

The book ends with a short essay written shortly after the conference by a dogmatic theologian, Raymund Schwager, a conference guest.

The book includes a foreword and bibliography written and compiled by Lohfink. The book does not pretend to be a comprehensive treatment of the theme but a beginning discussion by Catholic Old Testament scholars of a question thrust upon them by the present international scene.

It is significant that the conference and book received its impetus and direction not only from outside the field of Old Testament scholarship, but also of theological scholarship. Although the four essays are written by competent Old Testament scholars according to generally accepted historical-critical methods, the theory of violence developed by René Girard from his study of world literature, psychological analysis, ethnology and social theory provided the writers with new and better questions to ask of the Old Testament text. Without the provocation of Girard, the conference would never have happened. For the purpose of the conference his two important books were, <u>La violence et le sacre</u> (1972) and <u>Des choses chashées depius la fondation du monde</u> (1978).

Girard's theory is important to Old Testament studies in stating that violence is not merely one drive among many, but is above all that which separates humans from animals. Human greed gives birth to conflict which then moves toward violence. This original cause of conflict was soon lost to humanity and violence became blind. At the same time it was infectious and threatened humanity with chaos. To contain this chaos, all ancient societies developed the scapegoat mechanism which concentrated the aggressions of all upon one individual whom they considered guilty and who by this was destroyed. Over the cadaver of this person, the community came to peace. This took on religious significance in that the offering provided freedom from guilt and at the same time became the embodiment of the ones saved. In these two aspects was experienced the two aspects of the holy, Tremendum and Fascinosum. The experience was regularized in a repeated ritual of universal atonement which usually climaxed with a ritual meal, celebrating the new harmony of the community. By this mechanism, violence was ever and again contained.

Although Girard's viewpoint was essentially atheistic, in 1973 he wrote an essay claiming that only the Christian gospel did not follow the structure of all other religions on the point of violence. Unlike them, it does not cover up or veil the scapegoat mechanism by which violence was contained socially, but exposed it.

Girard's thought was introduced to German theological circles by the Catholic dogmatician, Raymund Schwager. Schwager saw Girard as the thinker by whom European spiritual development in consequence of its own logic and from its own presuppositions, had arrived where the evangelists had already stood some 2000 years ago, a period when humanity was not yet ripe for it. The Christian in a pluralistic society, Schwager held, was not to withdraw from society as a sect-type, nor to give up the faith by melting into the society, but was to be maintained by a "high faith consciousness" as a disciple of Jesus. Norbert Lohfink qualified Schwager's reception of Girard's thought somewhat (at a 1978 academic conference at Munich), saying that "we the disciples of Jesus sought to understand ourselves not in the 'heightened faith-consciousness' of individual Christians but in transformed, interdependent, powerless Christian congregations which stood as an alternative society to the universal society."

1. "Violence (Gewalt) as a Theme of Old Testament Research" (Lohfink)

Lohfink begins his history of research by pointing up that no other theme fills the OT like that of violence, giving statistics provided by Schwager. He points out that already in the second century Marcion saw this and responded by excluding the Old Testament from the canon. This solution is accepted today in a practical way by the recent exclusion of Psalms of violence from the Catholic lectionary. This solution, however, the church did not buy historically, holding, as did the New Testament, to the essential unity of both Testaments. Contrary to this self-evident fact of the predominant theme of violence, OT theologies do not deal with the theme, due, he thinks, to an unconscious mechanism at work which excludes everything dealing with violence.

After discussing secondary literature mainly known to us, Lohfink concludes that the question is discussed too narrowly. Is it anywhere discussed that violence is united with the legal order and the state, and that one cannot be discussed without the other? Can the problem of violence be discussed marginally, or must it come central to the discussion of the traditional themes of theology, especially since it is intricately involved in central Old Testament themes, such as the exodus, occupation, kingship, and eschatology?

It is interesting that Lohfink does not mention those Catholic orders which historically rejected the practice of violence. Also, his discussion of the Reformation includes the Lutheran and Reformed approaches, but omits entirely the Anabaptists. He includes some writings from Mennonite authors, but indicates that such writings were mostly unavailable to him. Norbert concludes the chapter by discussing the contribution to Old Testament scholarship from the outside, namely that of Girard and his disciples. He feels that no theory lightens up the meaning of OT texts like that of Girard.

2. "The Pentateuchal Sources and Warfare" (Lohfink)

Lohfink holds that there is an oriental commonality in regard to war which holds that divinity alone is the effective actor. J and E have a "natural" attitude toward war; warfare is not central but is accepted as a "fact of life." Although J consciously

excluded war from the patriarchal narratives, this may
have been because of their placement before the exodus
and occupation traditions, so that they could not have
been involved in the conquest.

Lohfink does not discuss why J omits war in the
primeval history.

Deuteronomy, on the other hand, shifts the weight
from the "natural" attitude of J and E to an
aggressive one. Lohfink regards Deuteronomy 1-Joshua
22 (DtrL) as essentially one source with two major
themes, conquest and law. Since these were the two
chief interests of Josiah, he assumes this to have
been written late in Josiah's reign as propaganda and
legitimation for Josiah's actions. (1) DtrL's theory
of holy war was that beside having faith, Israel was
to fight--as Lohfink notes, quite the opposite of
Isaiah 7:9 where faith for the prophet meant the
rejection of normal politics. (2) DtrL included the
special oath of **herem** as a part of warfare and then
generalized it to mean the destruction of the total
population. (3) DtrL had a juristic-theological
territorial concept: that God alloted to each nation
its land, which each nation then had to possess, as
receiver of a fief. This theory gave moral courage to
Josiah against Assyria. It united justice and power
in that justice is achieved by power and that behind
all stands divinity. This then was a charge from
older Israelite anti-state ideas to the legitimation
of state power, a charge which collapsed, however,
under the weight of the reality of Near Eastern
politics.

In contrast to J to whom war was "natural" and
certainly to DtrL to whom war was central to Yahwistic
faith, P omits warfare from its recounting of Israel's
history. "In the priestly historical narrative there
is no war." In this respect P resembles the
Chronicler who omits or even denies the conquest, not
because of a pacifistic interest (nowhere in the OT is
holy war so devotedly described as in the Chronicler),
but because of a bias of a mythological tendency to
link land and people from the time of creation. P
lacks war narratives entirely in Genesis. In the
Exodus Yahweh's judgment is substituted for war; the
Israelite camp in the wilderness was not at all a
military camp; the spy history had as its purpose to
divide the land which had been given as God's gift;
the instituting of Joshua was not a military action;
the entrance to Canaan was accomplished without an
army, God did it alone. God's judgment was tied to

This rejection of war by P was matched by a
construct of a world which functions without the use
of violence. P knows no state but assumes an
egalitarian, tribal enclave or sub-society gathered
around the Jerusalem temple. Holy war exists not
between humans but between humans and animals; the
inter-human peace is maintained by cultic ritual, the
scape-goat mechanism of animal sacrifice (Girard).
This absence of war is substituted by the presence of
the **kabôd** of Yahweh which consumes all that is
sinful.

This warless character of P is obscured by the
final redactor of the Pentateuch who unites the cultic
interest of P with the holy war interest of D as a way
of acting for the future (cf. Num 31; 32-34). Thus
the final Pentateuchal redaction qualifies the temple
society of P.

P, as noted above, is followed by the Chronicler
who rejected the conquest, by the Maccabees, and
especially by the Qumran Community which saw warfare
only as an eschatological event and that they
themselves were to live "pacifistically" in the
parenthesis. The basis for all this was the
Pentateuch, but the law rather than the narrative.
This then became the basis for Jesus' Sermon on the
Mount.

3. "Laments in Israel and Babylon: Different
Meanings of Power" (Ruppert).

In this essay, Ruppert compares laments mainly from
the Psalms which deal with the enemy and violence (Ps
109; 59; 10;7; 26; 27; 57; 142; 53, etc.) with the
most relevant Babylonian-Assyrian prayers of lament,
especially the Assyrian Maqlu collection (Maqlu I,
73-86; II, 38-49).

Although he finds an undeniable relationship
between the two religions, he rejects the earlier
results of Mowinckel and more lately of Vorländer and
Gerstenberger which by analogy with the Babylonian
laments identify the enemy with practitioners of magic
(hexers) and with demons. Comparison of religions is
valid, but ultimately each religion must be
interpreted within its own context. Ruppert concludes
that the setting of the Mesopotamian laments was
magic, while the Psalms had a wisdom setting.

In the Babylonian lament, sickness plays a major
role, in contrast with the laments of the Psalms which
are mainly directed at actions of the enemy. Since in
both cultures the natural causes of sickness were
unrecognized, numinous powers were regarded as

responsible. In Mesopotamia, (sickness) demons,
incited by hexers, could be warded off by sacrifices
which would propitiate an angered divinity. In
Israelite Psalms it was Yahweh's own self who caused
sickness, whether for punishment or for unknown
reasons, without the help of practitioners of magic
(hexers). The experience of sickness was essentially
demythologized in Israel, with the result that the
image of God, who alone was to be worshipped, took on
characteristics of the irrational (Job).

With this demythologizing also, the human
petitioners in the Psalms recognized much more clearly
than their Mesopotamian contemporaries that humans
were responsible for violence, perversion of justice,
and oppression in the inter-human and social arena.
In the Psalm lament, the enemies were mainly public
rather than private enemies, oppressors of the
socially weak, the poor who needed on their side to
trust in Yahweh, the God of justice (especially in the
later Psalms). Violence was the misuse of human
freedom. This means that the grotesque and demonic
was shifted almost exclusively to humans themselves,
especially to humans as sinners. In contrast to
Mesopotamia, violence was therefore considered not
merely as hostility to humans, but especially as
hostility directed against God. Because that is so,
violence, while it can be understood by the faithful,
can be overcome only by Yahweh's own self, by divine
judgment which creates justice for the threatened and
punishes the enemy, who opposes God's rule.

Statements which scandalize Christians from the
point of view of the Sermon on the Mount should be
seen in this light [perhaps they should be compared
with the woes of Jesus directed against those who do
not receive the gospel message?] In any case, they
are not (at least for the most part), to be regarded
as requests for personal vengeance, but as a cry of
the oppressed and powerless, that God might act to
redress injustice.

4. "The Message of the Servant of God: a Way to
Overcome Violence" (Haag)

In this section Haag deals with the four
traditional Servant Songs. He has a long section on
their literary criticism which results in a form
critical presentation of the four poems as one poem
made up of seven speeches, each with ten stichoi. He
regards this as the "basic stratum of the Ebed-Yahweh
Poem" which should be regarded as a literary whole
(unit), a "prophetic liturgy." His most radical

excision to achieve this remarkable result, is the removal of the two Yahweh speeches from Isaiah 53 (52:13-15; 53:12), ascribing them to a revision which in turn was later added to with "additions and supplements."

Haag deals with the tradition criticism of this "prophetic liturgy" by discussing the three speeches. He finds the poem dependent upon three traditions, the David tradition, the ancient tradition of the judges, and the deuteronomistic tradition of Jeremiah. The Davidic tradition was a deuteronomistic idealization of David developed in the exilic period. The Judges tradition had to do mainly with holy war elements of the poem, such as the "cry" of 42:2 (which the servant does not do) which he regards as the cry marshalling the militia, though the prophetic use of this cry marshalled the enemy of Israel. The Jeremiah tradition is credited as the background for the servant's non-violent reliance upon the word, which Haag traces especially to the deuteronomistic call of Jeremiah where this prophet of the word is placed over the nations. Also, Haag sees the statements of the opposition of the servant as influenced by Jeremiah's confessions.

Haag regards Deutero-Isaiah as author also of the Servant Poem. With a later redaction of Deutero-Isaiah, the Ebed-Yahweh poetry lost its original form. The biggest change was that the servant (originally an individual) was related not to Israel itself, but to the remnant saved by Yahweh, which then took on a collective meaning. The reason for the reinterpretation was the disillusionment suffered after the Exile when it was impossible to set up a Davidide, and therefore the message regarding the political structure was changed to one of an immediate theocracy.

The poem was a reflection begun in Israel's exile, caused by the fact that the Davidic mediator of Yahweh's rule no longer existed. This crisis, partly filled by the older prophetic authority, led to a continuing conversation regarding the reality and fulfillment of the theocracy and the destiny of the mediator.

Fundamental to this contribution is the unmasking of violence as an expression of sin and of the misuse of creation power, an unmasking accomplished by prophetic authority. This violence toward fellow humans is bound up with the lie (the opposite of a knowledge of God grounded on repentance) which like

violence is also an expression of sin. Because the
sinner has lost sight of the norm for a morally good
relation by rejection of God, in an attempt to
maintain him or herself as a sinner, he or she falls
under the delusion of violence. Instead of the hoped
for heightening of power this attempt brings only the
chaos of destruction and annihilation.

Salvation from violence is due to the divine
initiative, the work of salvation creating communion
with God, which sets aside the situation of sin, the
cause of the lie and violence. The effect of this new
saving communion with God is shown already in the
behavior of the divine servant who, confronting the
attack of violent sinners, does not imitate violence
nor vie with evil. The servant's decisive deed for
overcoming violence is vicarious atonement for the
sinner which is supported by God's self-communication
(Selbstmitteilung). This opposition the servant
recognized as directed as against God's own self, whom
the servant represented. However, when God personally
opposed the servant by making of the servant an
offering of vicarious atonement, this mediator no
longer stood before the violence of the sinner but
before God who enabled him by communication with God's
own self to complete his mission. At this point (Isa.
53), what astonishes the people is no longer the
rejection of violence but the servant's obedience
before God unto death. This unrestricted obedience
before God makes possible that rejection of violence
by the mediator, which constitutes his martyrdom.

Although Haag seems to hedge a bit about the right
of defense so that the Servant Songs are not a rule of
action valid for all cases, he does say that the
servant, while an individual of unique meaning, is at
the same time a representative of universal
obligation. The right to one's own self-assertion and
defense can only come under the scrutiny of the
highest norm, the revelation of the saving love of
God.

Evaluation

One can only rejoice that the Catholics are so
interested in peace that they call together a
conference of Old Testament scholars to discuss
violence and powerlessness. The participants in the
conference accepted the unity of the testaments as
well as their authority for the church today. The
matter of authority makes the violence of the Old
Testament a pressing matter.

While generally appreciative, I raise the following questions about their work:

1. The three authors are unanimous about their acceptance of the theory of Girard, though they all used the theory mainly to ask new questions of the biblical material. Does the theory, however, narrow the scope of their interest too narrowly to the issue of sacrifice. Can one relate this interest to the present Catholic emphasis on the mass?

2. Schwager complains about the amount of time given to textual criticism by the writers and the piece-meal results this tended to give. While I would not be critical of this per se, yet I feel that it is pushed beyond the limits of probability at certain points. Can we be sure that DtrL was oriented only to fit the political "needs" of the time of Josiah, that the **herem** had no basis in Israel's early history as a part of warfare, that P's rejection of warfare was obscured by a pentateuchal redactor who united P's ideas with those of DtrL? A differentiation of sources in the Pentateuch is difficult enough that one should not discredit the process by pushing the method to the point where it appears to be manipulation.

This is especially true of Haag where he radically alters the meaning of Isaiah 53 toward emphasis on vicarious atonement, effectively qualifying its political emphasis by removing the two Yahweh speeches.

But more important, the question beyond this is one of method. Does the tension of Yahweh's judgment and human violence lie essentially between the sources (DtrL and P, etc.), or is it found within each of the sources themselves? I would hold to the latter.

3. Lohfink is correct in saying that the question of violence should be seen more broadly in terms of structural violence, that violence is indissoluably connected with the state, and that both should be looked at together. It seems to me, however, that Girard's theory has distracted them from this broader approach.

4. Is Deuteronomy that well adapted to the power needs of Josiah? Why is the militia in the laws of warfare in no way connected to kingship? Why do these laws protect the voluntary status of the individual militiaman rather than emphasize the power needs of kingship? Above all, why is the king restricted as to army and wealth, and his "power base" made his obedience to Yahweh's word? These restrictions in praxis are accompanied by the doctrine that Israel is

powerless and must depend upon Yahweh for victory. The unity of this restrictive praxis with this doctrine makes the doctrine quite different from seemingly similar doctrines of other Near Eastern states.

5. The setting of the Psalms of violence within a wisdom rather than in a magical context (as in Babylon) is probably a correct understanding. The Christian is left, however, with the task of justifying these Psalms in light of the Sermon on the Mount.

6. Of the three essays, the final essay on the Servant Songs gave the greatest promise of unity with the New Testament. As noted above, the implication for the poet's attitude toward structural violence is blunted somewhat by the removal of the Yahweh speeches. Even more unfortunate is the tempering of the authority of the servant as a universal pattern by seeming legitimation of self-defense, a tempering which the New Testament does not do.

As stated above, these criticisms do not mean that I am unappreciative of the book. It is an important addition to a growing peace literature on the Old Testament.

PETER STUHLMACHER'S CONTRIBUTIONS
TO A BIBLICAL THEOLOGY OF THE NEW TESTAMENT

Paul Dyck

Introduction

Peter Stuhlmacher, Professor of New Testament at the University of Tübingen, has developed and advanced the thesis that the gospel of Jesus as Reconciler is at the heart of the New Testament. Stuhlmacher believes this thesis provides the foundation of a proposal for a unifying theme in biblical theology. Those concerned about the gospel of reconciliation and interested in finding a touchstone for unity in biblical theology therefore find his significant contributions to biblical scholarship to be of particular interest.

Unfortunately, very little of Stuhlmacher's work is available to the English reader. The following article will provide such a reader with a selective and highly condensed outline of Stuhlmacher's thought as contained in three of his recently published works: Das Evangelium von der Versöhnung in Christus; Vom Verstehen des Neuen Testaments; and Versöhnung, Gesetz, und Gerechtigkeit.

This article will follow Stuhlmacher's development of the Jesus as Reconciler theme. Particular attention will then be given to his treatment of the peace proclamation of Ephesians 2:14 and to his approach to a biblical theology. Finally I will offer a short response.

Stuhlmacher's Thesis: Jesus and Reconciliation

In the interests of efficiency, I will use a question/response format in this section and be bold enough to phrase the responses as if Stuhlmacher himself were responding. Stuhlmacher develops his thesis by answering the question 'Who was Jesus?' from the following three perspectives: 1) primitive Christian kerygma, ii) historical reconstruction, and iii) the NT texts.

Who was Jesus? Kerygma and Historical Reconstruction

The kerygma helps us discover what the earliest believers understood about Jesus. A NT theology must therefore remain closely tied to the kerygma. Two important kerygmatic texts help us in this endeavor: 1 Corinthians 15:3b-5 is the Jerusalem Credo which most scholarship acknowledges as the oldest transmission. Paul refers to it as the gospel.

Acts 10:34ff is Peter's sermon to Cornelius.
Together, these texts show how Jesus was spoken of
both in Jerusalem and in the mission setting; both
speak of Jesus as the promised Messiah. In Acts 10
Jesus' mission is described as that of bringing
salvation in the form of _peace_ between God and
humanity. This is the message of the OT prophets.
Both texts also agree that Jesus' death was the key
event, understood through the Isaiah 53 traditions of
repentance and substitution.

The Acts passage puts Jesus' mission in the light
of the prophetic promises of Isaiah 52:7 and Nahum
2:1. It shows how everything happened in Jesus'
earthly life so that he could be identified and
preached as the messianic Savior who offers salvation
of sins. Further, God's community of the end-time is
also announced and offered now (_Versöhnung_, p. 14).

Both kerygmatic passages recognize Jesus as the
Messiah, whose mission culminated in his death on the
cross. This death had the purpose of reconciling God
and humanity, that is, bringing peace between God and
humanity.

If we look back on Jesus' life, we see an amazing
congruence between the picture of Jesus developed
there, and the above kerygmatic profile.

Jesus was a reconciler. Many contemporary scholars
have noticed and worked with the fact that Jesus had
close relationships with the outcasts of society.
Bornkamm saw Jesus' table fellowship with sinners and
the poor and the suffering as a preview of the
communion of the Messiah. Conzelmann saw acceptance
of salvation and forgiveness of sin as the key to
Jesus' message in that Jesus called the poor and the
sinners to himself. Jeremias saw the heart of the
gospel in the proclamation of salvation to the poor.
Jesus' unconditional acceptance of the outcasts was at
the root of the conflict between Jesus and the
establishment. Other scholars say similar things. It
is evident that God is coming to the people in Jesus,
as Jesus is setting up the end-time rule of God, the
peace between God and humanity (_Versöhnung_, pp.
17-18).

Jesus was also the Messiah. We have a historical
picture of a proclaimer of the rule of God who stands
above and beyond all groups and classifications. In
fact, Jesus was in conflict with all the established
Jewish groups of his day. The Pharisees could not

tolerate Jesus' carelessness with their laws. The Zealots could not accept his call to love one's enemies, or his call to pay Caesar what is his. The Sadducees were threatened by his Temple cleansing, his word about the destruction of the Temple, and his giving of unconditional forgiveness. And the Romans, the Sanhedrin, and the Herodians, were all afraid of Jesus' political power because of his immense following in the general population.

This conflict was caused by Jesus' personification of the messianic reconciliation (Versöhnung, p. 19). Jesus' death was a foregone conclusion of his mission.

This profile of Jesus as a reconciling Messiah who had to die because of who he was, lines up closely to the kerygmatic profile formed above.

The understanding of Jesus' death and the nature of his Messiahship were not recognized (even by his disciples in Mark 8:27-33) until after Easter. The term Messiah carried different connotations of power in that day; often it referred to victorious, military, liberating power. The question about the messianic nature of Jesus followed him to the grave, and was resolved in the early kerygma.

Who is Jesus in the New Testament?

(Stulmacher accepts the position that all NT books were written before 100 A.D.: Evangelium, p. 32)

The basic content of the Pauline gospel is the word of reconciliation found in 2 Corinthians 5:18-20. The cross of Christ brings believers into righteousness, wisdom, holiness and redemption (1 Cor 1:1, 30; Evangelium, p 27).

It is clear, however, that Paul is not the first to speak about justification and reconciliation. The primitive Christian church had already formed these ideas. Paul utilizes these earlier Jerusalem traditions in passages such as Romans 3:25f, 4:25, and 1 Corinthians 15:3ff. In Romans 3:24-26 Paul uses phrases from the tradition that speak of Jesus' death as an atonement in which God's saving righteousness is revealed. In all probability this formulation comes out of the Stephen circle, which founded the church at Antioch and became Paul's base church. These ideas (also Rom 4:25) stem from the atonement offering tradition of Leviticus 16. The Day of Atonement was the highest act of the cult in post-exilic Israel. Through God's act of offering Jesus on the cross this atonement is now understood to have been accomplished

once and for all time. Now God is approachable. The
believer can now have access to God via the crucified
and risen Jesus. Romans 4:25 also links up with the
ideas of Isaiah 53; Jesus is the debt offering for our
sins, and for our justification he was raised from the
dead (Evangelium, p 27).

Paul made this atonement tradition the basis of his
justification gospel because he himself experienced
reconciliation and justification through Christ on the
road to Damascus. Here he was also liberated from the
law which bound all Jews. This liberation granted him
access to God, and meant becoming a servant of God.
This is the new creation of Paul. The new creation
enables one, and makes one responsible to live in
obedience to Jesus. Faith in Jesus the Reconciler is
identical with obedience to him.

Recognizing the reconciliation basis of Paul's
justification gospel solves the problem of the lack of
justification proclamation in Colossians and
Ephesians. In both of these letters the basic
reconciliation gospel is highlighted and developed
further.

James was written by Jesus' half-brother as a
circular writing, before his stoning in 62 A.D. This
letter does not emphasize, the reconciliation gospel.
Its works emphasis rather, is an attempt to remain
Jewish, to maintain the form of Jewish righteousness.
The insufficiency of his mode of Christianity is
revealed when, after James' stoning, the James circle
quickly develops into a sect. History clearly
pronounces its verdict on such a false emphasis. The
future of Christian growth and mission belongs to the
reconciliation gospel (Evangelium, p 31).

All three Pastorals have the same teaching content:
that is, to guard the treasure entrusted to you (2
Tim 1:14). This treasure or truth is Christ who was
vindicated by the Spirit (1 Tim 3:16). In the
pastorals, the goodness and people-friendliness of God
reveals Jesus as the Reconciler, and as such is the
content of true faith (Evangelium, p 32). Both
letters of Peter proclaim and defend the gospel of
reconciliation and justification.

Hebrews presents the problem of limiting the
offered reconciliation. Those who fall away from God
are excluded from reconciliation to him (6:4; 10:26).
In the Jewish understanding, under Leviticus 4, this
appears to mean that Christ's offering atones only for
humanity's fallen nature. It does not atone for its
voluntary dismissal of Christ's revelation. When

confronted with other scriptures (e.g. Rom 8:31-39),
we see how this, like James, is a vestige of
Torah-bound thinking. This is not thinking based
entirely in Christ (Evangelium, pp 33-35).

In his Gospel Mark basically follows Peter's Acts
10 sermon outline and fills in historical substance.
The center of Mark's gospel is the proclamation of
Jesus' messianic sonship of God. Jesus is the one who
with signs and wonders displays God's rule to the
lost. He fulfills the messianic task in that he gives
his life as a ransom for many (10:45). The basic
thrust is messianic. God reveals himself in Christ
and thereby establishes reconciliation with humanity.

Matthew sees Jesus in two ways. The first picture
is similar to the one in Mark, with the added idea
that Jesus, already from his birth, is the one who
will save God's people from sin (1:21-23). This is
Jesus the Messiah; he is the Son of God, sent by God,
and as such is the reconciler.

Matthew, however, also portrays a second view of
Christ, a view still bound by Jewish Torah-
consciousness. The Sermon on the Mount does not
foster the same complete, assured reliance on God's
atoning love in Christ on Judgment Day as does Romans
8:31. Here, Jesus goes beyond the Torah and erects a
new original law, expressing the will of God. In this
new system, only insofar as the church follows this
true will of God, this law of loving God and neighbor
including the enemy, is its righteousness better than
that of the scribes and Pharisees. Only those who
follow Jesus and abandon all else on earth, can appeal
to him.

This Gospel, with its obvious inner tension, was so
written because Matthew had to offer a defense against
accusations that Christians were scorners of the law,
as well as speak to enthusiastic Gentiles who were
forgetting God's love command (Evangelium, p 37).

Luke's Acts account is a collection of material
which is considered important some twenty years after
Paul died. The communication of Christ is the central
issue. Jesus is the gospel in person, the gospel that
grants access to God, especially for the poor. Jesus
is also the reconciler whose sacrifice makes community
possible. He is the perfect example who prays for his
crucifiers. This story is one of bringing God to the
people and bringing the people to God.

In the Gospels of Luke and John, Jesus is revealed
to be a reconciler who greets those who deserted him
with a peace greeting (Luke 24:36; John 20:19,21).

The disciples needed to re-encounter the risen Christ
in order to understand that they were (still) included
in the eschatological fellowship with Jesus, whose
reality they had already experienced with the earthly
Jesus (Versöhnung, p 25).

The Gospel of John is the work of the Johannine
circle after 70 A.D. It begins with the light of the
creation story; it ends with the light of the
resurrection glory. These lights are connected in
Jewish wisdom theology. The creation prologue calls
forth the image of wisdom as being the creation word
of God. The final words from the cross, 'It is
finished' refer to wisdom as the power of God that is
revealed on the Day of Atonement. Jesus is the
creating and revealing word of God in person. He
crowns his messianic commission of uniting God and
humanity in the act of giving up his life on the cross
(Evangelium, pp 40-41).

In the letters of John, the Johannine circle sees
Jesus' work as having been reconciliatory of 'our sins
and not ours only but also those of the whole world'
(1 John 2:2). God and his love are shown to be
available as 'God is love, and the one who abides in
love, abides in him' (1 John 4:16). As in the
Pastorals, these letters deal with heretical
teachings, and in both cases, the reconciler
christology is the anchor of the embattled faith.

Revelation was written by a primitive Christian
named John, who was not likely one of the twelve
apostles (21:14). The Christ of Revelation is the
wonderful reconciler, who stands against all powers in
support of those who remain true to him and who he
bought free. Revelation's center is the dawning of
God's rule through Jesus the Messiah (21:10ff). God's
rule is the heavenly Jerusalem, the fulfillment of
creation. There is no need for a temple here because
God and the Lamb live in the people and the people in
them. There is no room for the powers of chaos here
either because God has determined this end-time peace
for his creation. The reconciliation through Christ
aims precisely to this fulfillment of creation. It
becomes complete in the recreation of the entire
cosmos.

Did Jesus Understand Who He Was? (Mark 10:45)

If Mark 10:45 records the authentic words of Jesus,
we can conclude that Jesus knew and understood his
messianic calling and task. The majority of today's

biblical scholars, however, believe that these are not
authentic words of Christ (Versöhnung, p 27).
These scholars believe this is a post-Easter
construction of the early church. Pesch, for example,
argues that this verse is a joining together of two
traditions (coming to serve and coming as a ransom)
that do not naturally follow each other. It seems
they were joined together by someone other than Jesus.
The 'kai gar' which begins the verse (hosper' in
the Matt 20:28 parallel) also seems to indicate that
someone was using this connector to pull different
thoughts together, as opposed to reporting Jesus'
exact words.

The transmission of a quotation of Jesus' words,
however, can only be considered inauthentic when the
following two conditions are met: i) an earlier
synoptic parallel must use the same quotation without
using the Son of Man phrase, and ii) the thought
expressed must be contained in the thinking of the
early church. Neither of these conditions holds true
here. It appears that the early church, would, if
anything, refer to the exaltation of Christ, not to
his service (Versöhnung, p 35).

This is, then, a genuine saying of Jesus. This
opinion is strengthened when the source of this saying
is considered. Word studies that attempt to link this
quotation with Isaiah 53:10-12 lead to dead ends,
whether they reach back to the Hebrew or even the
Aramaic. The key word 'ransom' is missing, although
the conceptual relational idea is strong. There is,
however, a strong connection between Isaiah 43:3ff and
the Isaiah 53 text. In the former, Egypt is given by
God as a ransom for Israel. Jesus, who would have
been familiar with these texts, combined these two
Isaiah passages, and replaced Egypt with himself, to
come up with the statement we have in Mark 10:45
(Versöhnung, p 40).

How Is Jesus Our Peace? (Eph 2:11-18)
Ephesians 2:11-18 is an important passage that
brings the ideas of peace and reconciliation together.
Its exegesis is hotly debated, with many believing
this text was once part of a gnostic hymn. It is,
however, best seen as a christological exegesis of
Isaiah 57:19 (Eph 2:13, 17), Isaiah 9:5f (Eph 2:14),
and Isaiah 52:7 (Eph 2:17), utilizing rabbinic
hermeneutic. The main word eirene brings these
three Scriptures together in a typical Jewish manner.
The peace for those far and near (Isa 57:19) comes

through the messenger of peace (Isa 52:7). Jewish
sources recognize the messianic interpretation of
Isaiah 52:7 as well as the messianic relationship
between that text and Isaiah 9:5 (Versöhnung, p
234).

Ephesians interprets the Jewish exegesis
christologically. 'Those far away and those nearby'
refer to Gentiles and Jews. Peace refers to Jesus
himself, and Scripture is fulfilled in that Gentiles
and Jews work together for peace in the church. The
purpose of this text can be stated as the
reconciliation of Gentiles and Jews, through Jesus, to
God and to each other, in order to simultaneously make
visible both the miracle of the acceptance of the
Gentiles into the church and also the essential nature
of this church, which is the new reconciled people of
God (Versöhnung, p 234f).

The tensions between Jews and Gentiles were
particularly high after 70 A.D. when this letter was
written. This letter's message is to remind the
church that the real miracle and essence of the church
is that Jewish and Gentile Christians together form
the new people of God in which God's promises become
real. This message was needed at a time when
Jerusalem lay in ruins, making tensions especially
high. After all Gentiles had destroyed the Temple,
and Jews had a long history of hating Gentiles.
Conversely, Gentiles disliked Jews because of their
separateness, and because they always seemed to have
special privileges. Right into this complex situation
of division and animosity, Ephesians carries the
message of peace and reconciliation in Christ,
overcoming these divisions. This is a timely example
of where we find our peace (Versöhnung, p 241).

Stuhlmacher's Approach to Biblical Theology (NT)

Stuhlmacher sees the NT as one unified whole within
which tensions exist. He realizes that it is not a
completely unified whole, but strongly asserts that it
does not fall apart into conflicting traditions. He
believes a NT theology must include the essential
proclamation and faith traditions in one coherent
whole. He goes about doing this with the help of
historical judgment and systematic theological
evaluation. He seems to be reaching for a
synergistic, historically verifiable theological sum
of the NT's twenty-seven books. He believes it is
possible to discern a position on the unifying

substance of Christian faith, a position that leads
biblical theology forward.

The heart of the NT message (as described above),
and of Stuhlmacher's biblical theology, is the
reconciliation gospel. Stuhlmacher defends that core
message, as he outlines five demands of a biblical
theology of the NT. His first demand is that a
biblical theology correspond to the historical
realities of the Bible and the early church. The
preceding section shows how he satisfies that demand.

The second demand is to determine the relationship
between the Testaments in a true historical and also
dogmatically freeing way. Stuhlmacher believes that
today's many faceted and highly specialized biblical
scholarship has segregated the NT from the Old by
concentrating only on particular difficult texts,
thereby slighting the essential unity of the Bible.
He believes the OT belongs to the NT for historical
reasons as well as reasons of theme and content. He
goes so far as to say that the heart of the
reconciliation gospel dies when you separate the two
Testaments. The NT assumes from the start the
collective expositions about hope for reconciliation
and peace with God as the fulfillment of the OT
creation. Isaiah provides Stuhlmacher with his
longest list of connections but he sees other
prophetic strands anticipating the atonement as well;
he also cites priestly sources (Ezra 40-48, Lev
16-26), and notes that the sacrificial cult points
also to Jesus (Evangelium, p 45). The Torah
tradition, via its close connection to Israel's wisdom
theology, is seen also as important to the NT as are
the Psalms.

The OT gave the NT its language. The OT makes it
possible to speak of reconciliation, justification and
other elements of God's kingdom. Conversely, the
gospel of Christ appears as the fulfillment of the
language of the OT. It is the messianic-hoped-for
reality of God's rule of his community and fellowship
(Evangelium, p 35).

Stuhlmacher believes the Testaments belong close
together. They are the canon of which Jesus is the
theological criteria. However, it is necessary for
the OT to recognize its own Messiah, and a biblical
theology of the NT must focus the question of Jesus'
Messianic-identity (Evangelium, p 47).

Stuhlmacher's third demand for a biblical theology
of the NT is that it identify lines of uniformity in
salvation thought; it must make precise statements

about how the NT books relate to each other. He views
the NT as a broad, historically differentiated
proclamation of the reconciliation whose central
message holds together its diversities. He
understands the diversity and tensions as historical
guideposts encountered en route to a completed
language of the reconciliation gospel. He emphasizes
the recognition of the centrality of Jesus the
Reconciler to the point of making it the criteria that
judges whether a particular scripture is central to
the canon or only secondary (Evangelium, p 49).

Stuhlmacher's fourth demand for a biblical theology
of the NT concerns its relationship with the church.
Stuhlmacher believes that theology is the science of
the church and should serve the Bible-believing
church. University theology cannot work against the
church's mission responsibility; both ought to
strengthen and support each other (Evangelium, p
5-6). He sees the church's task as that of witnessing
to the reconciliation it experiences as it hopes for
the fulfillment of that reconciliation in the future
rule of God. The Christian witness of faith is
derived from the revelation of the reconciliation
gospel. This gospel motivates us not to be resigned
about, but affirming of our biblical foundation,
confessional ties, and present tasks.

Stuhlmacher's final demand is to remain in
communication with biblical scholarship. He believes
it is possible to construct a NT theology that is
helpful in dealing with present difficulties in
scholarship and in the church. He has constructed his
theology on the basis of careful and disciplined
scholarship. He is openly critical of radical
biblical criticism that has contributed nothing
constructive, but has rather occupied itself with
shattering things and making them incomprehensible
(Evangelium, p 52).

Stuhlmacher believes more responsibility is needed
on the part of the scholars. Biblical scholarship
must learn how to be discriminating in the use of
methods of textual analysis. It must learn how to be
as historically complete as possible. He insists that
to be critical in the historical realm means to seek
the truth of the reality that is there to see, that
is, the actual text (Evangelium, p 50-52).

The Jesus event, in word and deed, is seen in this
NT theology as presenting Jesus as the messianic
reconciler, whom he knew himself to be, and whom he
became via the power (gained from God) of his death

and resurrection for believers. Jesus worked and suffered as the incarnated reconciling word of God. The primitive Christians recognized this and proclaimed Jesus to be the messianic reconciler.

Short Response

I appreciated both Stuhlmacher's method and his message. He has a strong commitment to rigorous exegesis and combines this with a historical realism that produces a convincing picture of solid theology. He does not build a case from one conjecture to the next, but begins with a solid footing in the Scriptures, and ties as much as he can concretely to them. I also agree that Jesus' earthly life speaks of his messianic purpose of reconciliation. Stuhlmacher's message about Christ was closely linked to who he saw Jesus to be and what he saw Jesus doing. This sort of immediacy was also gained by working through the NT and identifying the messianic theme of reconciliation.

I also support his point that the content of the gospel shows Jesus as messianic reconciler. This is certainly a key way of seeing Jesus, who he was and what he accomplished and is accomplishing.

However, I have some misgivings about Stuhlmacher's thought as I understand it. Stuhlmacher seems to believe he needs to establish a definitive core truth of the gospel. He distills a single message out of the Bible. His theology has a "closed system" flavor that may be putting Jesus into a too rigid form. Although he admits there are tensions in the Bible, he makes one central truth outrank them by demoting certain sources. It is thus necessary for him to demote those Scriptures which he considers to be Torah-bound (James, Hebrews, and the Sermon on the Mount). This may not seem so surprising when we consider Stuhlmacher's context: his German setting and his battle with radical biblical scholarship. Yet it is particularly painful when it is applied to the Sermon on the Mount, which is a core Scripture in Anabaptist-Mennonite tradition. I believe Stuhlmacher is wrong when he sees the Sermon's most radically right-side-up Christian teaching to be, at best, a misrepresentation of the true Christian view of things.

This leads me to Stuhlmacher's lack of regard for the issue of discipleship. He alludes to it when he states that Paul equates faith with obedience, and

when he speaks of the church and peace in the world.
But these are merely hints. Particularly with regard
to peace, this is an area of significant weakness in
his theology. Peace after all is a discipleship
issue. It is more than a cozy, assured relationship
with God through Christ; it is a way of living.
Although Stuhlmacher does explain that peace needs to
be thought of in relation to our neighbors (in the
church at least), he leaves the impression that this
is something that is done for us (as God brings about
the fulfillment of his creation) and not by us. What
is our ministry of reconciliation (2 Cor 5:18, 19) and
of peace?

In summation, despite solid scholarship, clear
methodology, biblical unity, and a powerful message of
messianic reconciliation, Stuhlmacher's sketch of a
biblical theology of the NT is in need of revision.
It needs to acknowledge the messages of Scripture it
has squeezed out of the way; it needs to recognize
that any faithful biblical theology will identify and
creatively deal with the tensions in the Bible; and it
needs to step out into the world and guide the church
toward true discipleship.

Jesus as Conscientizer

- Jan Lugibihl

The thesis of this paper is that if one uses the model delineated in Paulo Freire's Pedagogy of the Oppressed, Jesus may be seen as the ultimate conscientizer. His method of leadership and living model both praxis and humanization in ways that continue to speak to us if we allow them to do so.

A word must be said here about method. It is, perhaps, risky to try to use a book written two thousand years after Jesus lived to prove something about him or to categorize him; however, it seems possible that Freire's method can help us discover a different way of seeing Jesus. The approach of this paper, therefore, will not be to prove that Freire had Jesus in mind when he wrote the book, but rather that Freire's insights into pedagogy might help us better understand what Jesus did when he lived and the impact his life and message continue to have today.

First, Freire's ideas will be briefly outlined, then the words and actions of Jesus will be used to show how this model might be applied to him. Because the purpose of this paper is to show how Jesus' being affected the lives of ordinary people, commentaries have not been used. Instead, an effort will be made to enter the situation as if we were participants in it. Finally, some of the ways in which it seems Jesus was and is more than the kind of conscientizing force Freire describes will be pointed out.

Freire describes conscientization in the following way:

> Men emerge from their submersion and acquire the ability to intervene in reality as it is unveiled. Intervention in reality—historical awareness itself—thus represents a step forward from emergence, and results from the conscientizacão of the situation. Conscientizacão is the deepening of the attitude of awareness characteristic of all emergence.[1]

This conscientization, then, occurs as people become aware of their concrete situation, and also of the possibility of moving beyond that state, of transforming it. When people become aware of "the situations which limit them: the "limit-situations'"[2] they respond with "'limit-acts': those directed at negating and overcoming, rather than passively accepting, the 'given.'"[3] When a particular limit-act is successful and one limit-situation is overcome, a new one will arise to take its place and so the cycle continues.

Further, the collection of limit-situations in a particular historical epoch together form the "generative themes"[4] of that time in history. Often the themes of a particular epoch are in dialectical contradiction to each other. Also, "limit-situations imply the existence of persons who are directly or indirectly served by these situations and of those who are negated and curbed by them."[5] To illustrate, Freire says that the fundamental theme of our epoch is domination, which implies liberation as the objective to be worked for.[6]

The problem, then, is to help people find ways to "de-code" their reality. "And in the way they think about and face the world--fatalistically, dynamically, or statically--their generative themes may be found."[7]

It is here that the role of the conscientizer becomes critical. S/he must help people realize "the reality of oppression not as a closed world from which there is no exit, but as a limiting situation which they can transform."[8]

In order to do this, the leader must enter the reality of the oppressed. Conscientization cannot occur in a hierarchical model, but must be done from within the historical situation, in solidarity with the oppressed:

> The revolution is made neither by the
> leaders for the people, nor by the people
> for the leaders, but by both acting
> together in unshakable solidarity. This
> solidarity is born only when the leaders
> witness to it by their humble, loving,
> and courageous encounter with the
> people.[9]

Leaders must enter into solidarity out of love for the oppressed and with a desire for the humanization of all. They must trust in the transformative power of people who have been made aware of their situation, and must be able to instill in the people the necessity for struggle and the importance of dialogue and communion. The dialogue cannot exist without hope, however:

> Hope is rooted in men's incompletion,
> from which they move out in constant
> search--a search that can be carried out
> only in communion with other men.[10]

The tools of the conscientizing leader include this
dialogue, but center on praxis--"the praxis which, as
the reflection and action which truly transform
reality, is the source of knowledge and
creativity."[11]   Again, praxis is only authentic when
both the leader and the people are active participants
in it. It also must include both action and
reflection, for action without reflection becomes
activism and reflection without action becomes
verbalism.[12]

The conscientizer must also be aware of the
dynamics of oppression. Primary among these is the
fear of freedom "which may equally well lead them to
desire the role of oppressor or bind them to the role
of oppressed."[13]

Another dynamic is that the oppressors can never
free themselves or others. Too much self-interest is
involved. Only as the oppressed struggle and free
themselves will the oppressor become liberated. "To
the oppressor consciousness, the humanization of the
'others,' of the people, appears not as the pursuit of
full humanity, but as subversion."[14]

The conscientizer must be fully aware of the power
of the word and that "there is no true word that is
not at the same time a praxis.[15] Thus, to speak a true
word is to transform the world."

In addition, the leader must realize the potential
risk of his/her actions. For instance:

> any populist leader who moves (even
> discreetly) towards the people in any way
> other than as the intermediary of the
> oligarchies will be curbed by the
> latter--if they have sufficient force to
> stop him.[16]

The leader must also continuously keep in mind
his/her need to develop a community with the
oppressed, for only with such an action can
transformation occur. The leaders and the people must
see themselves as objects, rather than subjects for
true conscientization to occur.

> . . . the leaders . . . do not own the
> people and have no right to steer people
> blindly towards their salvation. Such a
> salvation would be a mere gift from the
> leaders to the people--a breaking of the

> dialogical bond between them, and a
> reducing of the people from co-authors of
> liberating action into the objects of
> this action.[17]

Through the entire process of conscientization, the
leaders provide a witness to the people, a witness
that may not always be immediately accepted by the
oppressed. Leaders must bear in mind the elements of
this witness.

> The essential elements of witness which
> do not vary historically include:
> consistency between words and actions;
> boldness which urges the witness to
> confront existence as a permanent risk;
> radicalization (not sectarianism)
> leading both the witnesses and the ones
> receiving that witness to increasing
> action; courage to love . . .; and
> faith in the people, since it is to
> them that authentic witness is made
> . . . .[18]

These are the primary components of conscientized
living as outlined by Freire. How, then, does Jesus
fit into and move beyond this model? To help
determine this, we will examine specific words and
actions of Jesus which may have planted a
conscientizing seed in the minds of the people whose
lives he touched. Finally, some ways in which Jesus
went beyond the methods proposed by Freire will be
examined.

First, it may be helpful to outline some of the
limit-situations operative in the world in which Jesus
lived and worked. A primary aspect of the time seems
to be that all parts of life were circumscribed by
law, religious and civil. For example, the Pharisees
had managed to make people believe that to be pleasing
to God they had to imitate them. They thus created in
the people a guilt complex which made them docile
subjects, easily dominated by the Pharisees.[19]

To whom one could relate and in what way was
determined by religious law. Women, gentiles, the
sick, and the poor--the life of each of these
marginalized groups was to be treated in specific
ways, ways that denied to them the right to be objects
in their own transformation and dehumanized them.

In addition, Roman domination was a reality that
colored the lives of all Jews. According to Cassidy,
"the fundamental premise on which the Roman empire
rested was that other peoples were to be subjugated

and controlled by force."[20]   Further, the Romans
had, by giving power to the Sanhedrin, enlisted Jewish
religious leaders in furthering their empire's
aims.[21]

It was into this world that Jesus came as
conscientizer. He spent thirty years living among the
people before he began his public work and in that
time undoubtedly became aware of and perhaps
experienced the oppression and dehumanization they
were feeling. According to Mateos, there were
basically only two economic classes in Palestine at
the time Jesus lived--the poor and the well-to-do land
owners.[22]   Given the fact that Jesus was a
carpenter's son, it is most likely that he grew up in
the peasant class with the awareness of the
limit-situations inherent in it: ". . . there was no
hope of human promotion for the poor, and they had no
means of bettering their situations, which depended
wholly on the will of the men in power."[23]

If the oppression of the marginalized was, indeed,
a generative theme of the epoch, then the dialogical
opposite would have been liberation for those people.
It is with this in mind that Jesus' agenda for his
work must be read:

> The Spirit of the Lord is upon me,
> because he has anointed me to preach good
> news to the poor. He has sent me to
> proclaim release to the captives and
> recovering of sight to the blind, to set
> at liberty those who are oppressed, to
> proclaim the acceptable year of the Lord.
> (Luke 4:8-10,RSV)

With this word, consciously chosen, Jesus set the
stage for the praxis he would follow.

Next, Jesus selected a group of disciples with whom
to live and act in communion. He forced no one to
join the group which included persons from among the
marginalized. "Jesus did not form a closed group but
an open one that had to grow, drawing men and women to
the new style of life that he was going to teach his
first disciples."[24]

Once he had chosen his disciples and articulated
his plan, Jesus began to act in a conscientizing
praxis. He did this by humanizing people, at risk to
himself. "Liberation for people's oppressed
consciousness can be sensed in all Jesus' attitudes
and words. The people perceive it and are deeply
stirred. The authorities grow panicky."[25]

Three accounts of Jesus' praxis will help to
illuminate this conscientizing of the marginalized.
First, the account in the fourth chapter of John of
Jesus' meeting with a Samaritan woman (John 4:4-42).
Jesus was resting by a well and a Samaritan woman came
to get water. He spoke to her, asked her for a drink
of water and then revealed to her the fact that he is
the Messiah. He also told her what he knew about her
life, but did not judge her. Even his disciples did
not understand what he was doing. She was a Samaritan
and, as she herself said, "Jews have no dealings with
Samaritans." (v. 9) Because she was a woman, the fact
that Jesus talked with her and accepted a drink from
her was even more unusual. "She was considered
ritually unclean since customarily Jews considered
Samaritan women as menstruants (and hence unclean:
Lev. 15:19) from their cradle!"[26] When she left,
she returned to her village and told everyone what had
happened, and her testimony convinced them to believe.

Because Jesus responded to her as a human being,
not as one member of some category, she became aware
of her situation--she was conscientized--and was able
to emerge from it and witness to what had happened to
her. A seed of hope had been planted in her. She
shared it with others, and perhaps it grew:

I remember it as if it were yesterday, but it
must have been two years ago now. I was sitting
by my house, making a new basket, when, all of a
sudden I heard a commotion down the road. I
looked up and saw Mary running toward me,
shouting something I couldn't understand at
first. Finally I got her calmed down enough to
talk clearly. She said a man, a Jew, had been at
the well and he spoke to her and even took water
from her. I thought she had gone crazy--no good
Jew would ever do that. Mary insisted it had
happened. Then she said something even stranger:
he had told her how many husbands she's had and
that she was living with someone who is not her
husband. When she said that, I was sure she had
had too much sun. How would anyone, especially a
Jew who had never been to our village, know all
that? Then, to top it all off, Mary said he had
told her he was the Messiah. When she said that,
I got scared for her. If the wrong people heard
her talking like that, she could be in real
trouble.

I made her go away--I'm ashamed to say it
now--and I went into my house. When John came

home a little later, he said most of the people
in the town believed Mary and some of them had
invited the Jew—Jesus was his name--to stay in
the town. I was frightened. I didn't want some
man I'd never seen before telling me what I've
done in my life, so for the whole first day he
was here I stayed inside my house.

But I started thinking. I thought a lot about
Mary--she had looked different the day before, as
if she had been given a gift. And I began to
realize that, in a way, she had. Most of the
Jews we see and all of the men treat us Samaritan
women as less than human, as if we don't have
minds or feelings. But this man not only talked
to Mary, he told her he was the Messiah. I still
wasn't ready to believe that was true, but even
if he wasn't, he was still very different from
any man I knew. So, I went to see him. I stood
at the back of the crowd, but I heard him say the
same things he had said to Mary at the well--that
he had water to give, water like a spring flowing
to eternal life. He didn't say he was the
Messiah again, though.

It's been two years now and I'm still not
certain about all that happened. I know that
Mary has been different--surer of herself,
somehow. And I know that I think about his being
here a lot. I don't know if he's the Messiah,
but, what if he is and the only person he told
here is my sister Mary?

A second example of Jesus' conscientizing praxis
can be found in the numerous stories of his reclaiming
of the Sabbath for humanizing purposes. One such
account is found in Mark 3:1-6. One Sabbath, Jesus
cured a man with a withered hand to show that it is
good, it is humanizing, to care more for life than for
rules. According to Mark, the Pharisees immediately
joined forces with the Herodians to find ways to
destroy him.

This response indicates that Jesus' action had
threatened the Pharisees. If, as Mateos suggests, the
Pharisees' insistence on the letter of the law meant
that an "excessive carefulness in small matters
concealed a glossing over of the really important
things."[27] then Jesus' question which silenced them
(v. 4), as well as the healing act itself threatened
their hold on the people by exposing their interest in
the law at the expense of human beings.

Jesus, instead, embodied a concern for humanization
that would eventually lead him to his death:

> . . . Jesus establishes a new praxis,
> whose axis is service to and love of the
> other. This praxis is bound to put on
> guard the power-wielders, who have much
> to do with any oppression or domination.
> Love of neighbor becomes political
> practice. The first case is that of
> Jesus himself: for having initiated and
> proclaimed a praxis of conscientization
> and salvation, he drew upon himself all
> the ire of the Jewish authorities. .[28]

Last week on the Sabbath I was in the
synagogue and this man Jesus who everyone has
been talking about came in. Benjamin, with the
crippled hand, was there as he always is. Jesus
called him over. We all watched to see what he
would do. At first, all he did was ask the
Pharisees a question about what it's right to do
on the Sabbath--good or evil. They didn't say
anything, but I could see how angry they were
that he had tricked them. Before anyone knew it,
Jesus healed Benjamin's hand. That was an
amazing thing for all of us to see and I know it
made the Pharisees even more angry.

I haven't stopped thinking about it since.
Why would Jesus heal Benjamin whom he didn't even
know and risk making the Pharisees angry? He
must know how powerful they are. I've been
thinking about something else, too. Why do we do
exactly as the Pharisees tell us? Some of the
things they say are in the law seem silly. When
I went to the synagogue this week I listened hard
to the reading from the law and I heard things
I've never heard before--not rules to follow,
something else. I think what I heard is that God
cares about me living a full life. God isn't so
concerned that I follow every rule. God's real
wish for me is that I love my neighbors. If
that's true, I need to make some changes in how
I'm living. I'm not sure about any of this. I'm
going to talk to my friends to see what they
think.

A third account, the story of Zacchaeus (Luke
19:1-10), points out Jesus' concern for the poor. In
this account, Jesus invited himself to the house of
Zacchaeus, a tax collector. The important point of
the story is not Zacchaeus' occupation, but the fact

that on that day he gave half of what he owned to the
poor. For this action in solidarity with the poor,
Jesus rewarded Zacchaeus with the news that he had
been saved. The conscientizing dynamics of this event
are several. First, Jesus' response to Zacchaeus'
action must have spoken to others who were rich; and
second, the poor people who heard the story or
benefitted from Zacchaeus' act would have been given
much to think about, also.

Last month one day I was in my house wondering
where I was going to find food to feed the
children, when a stranger came to the door. He
was dressed in fine clothes. At first I was
frightened. Why would someone like that come to
see me unless I had done something wrong?

When I recognized him, it was even worse. He
was Zacchaeus, the tax collector. I didn't have
any money and I had no idea where I would find
any. He must have noticed I was afraid because
he told me not to worry. He said he was there to
give me money, not to take it from me. I
thought it was some new trick of the authorities.

But then he told me he was doing this because
of a man named Jesus. I still didn't believe
him--why would anyone give away money just
because someone else told him to? Zacchaeus said
he wasn't sure he understood it himself, but
there was something about Jesus. The words he
said, but more than that, his presence.
Zacchaeus said Jesus had told him he was saved
because he was giving his money away and that
Jesus, himself, lived like a poor man, but spoke
words of life and hope. That Jesus really cared
about people and that there was something almost
holy about him.

I took what Zacchaeus offered--God knows we
need it--even though I was still suspicious.
Since then I've tried to find out more about
Jesus. He does live like a poor man. And he
heals people and tells wonderful stories. People
say there's something about him that makes you
feel like he knows you and cares about you even
if he doesn't talk to you. He's not afraid of
the authorities, either. He asks them questions
they can't answer and does things that break the
law, but help people.

I don't know if I believe all of that, but I
wonder about someone who can get a man as rich as
Zacchaeus to give half of his money away without

using physical force. Why would Jesus even care
if there are poor people--no one else seems to.
Maybe I should find out more about him. Maybe I
should even try to see him. But first, Zacchaeus
gave me so much, I want to share some of it.

These three examples of Jesus' praxis focus
specifically on his concern for the marginalized of
his society. There are many more examples, of course,
of the way in which Jesus' everyday actions humanized
the people around him. The parables, for instance,
are excellent examples of the manner in which Jesus
used words to create the beginnings of awareness in
people--to conscientize them.

What he did he grounded always in the idea of love
of neighbor. He did not lose faith in the people, nor
did he abandon them. He lived in total solidarity
with them.

> Only on the basis of this identification
> could he carry out the work of
> liberation. Jesus had the experience of
> being marginalized, denounced, accused,
> and plotted against by the centers of
> power. He had no structural or
> institutional defense. He always moved
> about at the grassroots level.[29]

As this quotation implies, Jesus was aware of what
might happen to him as a result of his solidarity with
the poor, yet he continued to speak the liberating
word to them. He continued the rhythm of action
(miracles, sermons, dialogues) and reflection (going
away from the crowds to pray) that formed his
conscientizing praxis. He continued to show his
belief and faith in the people. He continued to
dialogue with oppressor and oppressed alike. Jesus
did all of this, not only because he believed in the
people, but because of his awareness of himself as
God's child and messenger. It is this awareness that
moves Jesus beyond Freire's model of conscientizer.

Perhaps in addition to saying Jesus was/is the
ultimate conscientizer, it is also necessary to say
that he was more conscientized than any other child of
God has been or is. He never lost his awareness of
himself as God's child, as we sometimes seem to lose
ours. Nor did he lose sight of his mission, his
vocation, as Croatto would call it:

> At the time of his anointing by the
> Spirit, Jesus was consecrated for the
> vocation of the "suffering Servant." And
> this vocation took explicit shape in his

life, through his actions and his word,
coming to fruition in his death-
resurrection.[30]

The death of Jesus and his resurrection are,
perhaps, the ultimate acts of conscientization.
Freire speaks of the need for leaders to be willing to
risk death. But God, through Jesus, moves one giant
step further. Jesus, in his praxis during his life,
gives people a living image of the kingdom of God, but
God, in the ultimate conscientizing praxis--the
ultimate bringing together of word and action--ensures
that people forever will have to confront the
possibility of the kingdom of God happening for them
and through them right where they are living.

Today I talked to Mary, one of the women who
had been closest to Jesus. She told me something
I could hardly believe, except that Mary has
never lied to me before. We had been together at
Jesus' crucifixion and I had gone home after it,
sad and angry. I had been filled with such hope
by all the things I had seen him do and heard him
say. I felt betrayed--he was only human, after
all, someone they could destroy in the end as
they have destroyed all of us through the years.
I felt stupid that I had believed he was
different--that his life would make a difference
in the world.

Anyway, Mary told me she had gone to the
garden where he had been buried and found the
tomb was empty. I felt awful. They would not
even let his body rest. But Mary looked radiant
when she told me, not sad, so I asked her to
explain. She said that first, in the garden, an
angel had come to her, and then Jesus
himself--alive!

I'm not sure why, but I believe her. And now
I think that all the things he said and did may
not be forgotten. The kingdom of God he promised
may really come. I think I must get my friends
together and convince them of the truth of Mary's
words and together we must find a way to make
sure no one forgets. We can do it! We can
make the kingdom come, if we only remember and
live the memory.

In the process of researching and writing I have
become aware of the reality of conscientization. All
I have known and felt of Jesus in the past has been
inside me, germinating. And now I wonder if I can

begin to see some green, new life. A stirring of
hope.

The vignettes included in this paper are more than
an attempt to re-create what might have happened in
the lives of the people around Jesus, they are
episodes in my own conscientizing. I am in the midst
of the process outlined in <u>The Pedagogy of the
Oppressed</u> and there is fear, but also a sense of hope
in that awareness.

Notes

1. Paulo Freire, _Pedagogy of the Oppressed_, trans. by Myra Bergman Ramos (New York: Continuum, 1982), pp. 100-101. Male language has not been changed when it is found in the original source.

2. Ibid., p. 89.

3. Ibid.

4. Ibid., p. 92.

5. Ibid.

6. Ibid., p. 93.

7. Ibid., p. 97.

8. Ibid., p. 34.

9. Ibid., p. 124.

10. Ibid., p. 80.

11. Ibid., p. 91.

12. Ibid., p. 75.

13. Ibid., p. 31.

14. Ibid., p. 45.

15. Ibid., p. 75.

16. Ibid., p. 149.

17. Ibid., p. 168.

18. Ibid., p. 177.

19. , Juan Mateos, "The Message of Jesus," _Sojourners_ (July, 1977), p. 2.

20. Richard J. Cassidy, _Jesus, Politics and Society: A Study of Luke's Gospel_ (Maryknoll, N.Y.: Orbis Books, 1978), p. 55.

21. Ibid., p. 50.

22. Mateos, "The Message of Jesus," p. 4.

23. Ibid., p. 3.

24. Ibid., pp. 2-3.

25. Leonardo Boff, "Christ's Liberation via Oppression: An Attempt at Theological Construction from the Standpoint of Latin America." _Frontiers of Theology in Latin America_, ed. Rosino Gibellini (Maryknoll, N.Y.: Orbis Books, 1979), p. 118.

26. Leonard Swidler, _Biblical Affirmations of Women_ (Philadelphia: Westminster Press, 1979), p. 189.

27. Mateos, "The Message of Jesus," p. 3.

28. J. Severino Croatto, _Exodus: A Hermeneutics of Freedom_, trans. by Salvator Attanasio (Maryknoll, N.Y.: Orbis Books, 1981), p. 63.

29. Ibid., p. 51.

30. Ibid., p. 77.

THE NEW LAW OF CHRIST AND EARLY CHRISTIAN PACIFISM

William L. Elster©

Introduction

"The New Testament is as barren of references to wars as the Old Testament is replete, hence New Testament teachings on warfare and related matters could lead to equivocal conclusions."[1] This statement aptly describes the dilemma with which many readers of the Scriptures are presented when they attempt to find a ruling in the New Testament that permits or prohibits Christians from serving in the military. In the canonized texts, no direct statement on this topic had been recorded either by Jesus or by the New Testament writers. Consequently, the writings of the early church writers are consulted to discover what their views were on this question. If it was found that they held a common point of view on this subject, perhaps that would provide Christians with a clue as to what the position of Jesus and the apostles could have been on this issue.

Unfortunately, scholars who have studied the patristics' attitudes toward war and the military have reached opposite conclusions. Most agree that only a small number of Christians served in the Roman legions for the first three hundred years of Christianity, but they disagree on why this was so. Some think that the Christians stayed out of the armed forces because they did not want to take part in the idolatrous ceremonies that were practiced by the Roman military, but that when that obstacle was removed, so was the church's opposition to the army. Other scholars have argued that most of the early Christians refused to join the army because they rejected committing acts of violence per se.[2]

The purpose of this paper is to show that the early Christian writers believed in a doctrine known as the New Law of Christ, and that it was used in a number of their statements which explained why they believed Christians should not participate in wars. This will be done by examining the most indicative quotations penned by Christian writers who before the year 313 A.D. wrote on the New Law. It will be noticed that sometimes these authors will use different titles, such as the Eternal Law, the Second Law, or the Final Law. These are all synonyms for the New Law.

There are two reasons why the cutoff date of 313 A.D. was chosen. The first reason is that during this time a change occurred in the legal status of

108

Christianity in the Roman Empire. In that year the so-called Edict of Milan was issued by the Roman co-emperors Constantine and Licinius. The edict for the first time placed Christianity, as well as other faiths, in the status of legal religions. This was the first step in the process of elevating Christianity to the status of the only official Roman state religion by c. 391 A.D. This change in the relationship between the state and the church most probably resulted in the change of the church's attitude toward military participation.

The second reason was that after perusal of the post-Necene writings, it became evident to me that the amount of literature making mention of the New Law of Christ significantly decreased. Yet, as I hope to show in this paper's conclusion, it appears that the knowledge of this doctrine by Christians after this period continued.

The doctrine of the New Law will be reviewed in a chronological method. That is, the patristical literature will be separated into five divisions: 1) the apostolic period; 2) the apologetical works of the mid-second century A.D.; 3) the anti-heretical works of the late second century A.D.; 4) the writers of the third century A.D.; and 5) the early fourth century A.D. Latin writers. Afterwards, some conclusions will be discussed.

One caution should be noted. Even if it was found that many of the church fathers agreed that Christians should not join the army on the basis of the New Law of Christ, this would not prove that a large majority of Christians shared this belief. For in studying the patristics, "the putative connection between literary statement and actual Christian practice needs to be carefully weighed."[3] Having stated this caveat, the study of the ante-Nicene writers' attitudes on the New Law of Christ can now proceed.

The Apostolic Writers

The earliest Christian writings were the gospels and the church epistles. By 90 A.D. the letters of Paul were collected and published together. From this time, letter writing became a standardized literary type for Christians.[4] In our study of the New Law of Christ in the apostolic period, two letters and a book of revelations will be reviewed.

Some of the most famous letters from this period are the ones Ignatius, the bishop of Antioch, wrote to five churches in Asia Minor. Ignatius (d.c. 107 A.D.) wrote these messages as he was being taken to Rome to be executed. His letters warn the believers to beware of heresies, such as Docetism, and to maintain their church's unity, with the bishop acting as its head and center.

This was his message To the Church at Magensia. Ignatius exhorted the Christians to render full respect to their youthful bishop. "As wise men yield to him--not to him but to the Father of Jesus, to the bishop of all."[5] He commended the deacon Zotian who remained "...subject to the bishop as to God's grace and to the presbytery as to the law of Jesus Christ."[6] Ignatius did not explain what he thought the phrase "the law of Jesus Christ" meant. Possibly he was just repeating what Paul wrote in some of his epistles (1 Cor. 9:21, Gal. 6:2). Ignatius' desire was to imitate Paul as an elder, as a writer, and as a martyr.[7] Yet, could there have been a teaching called "the law of Jesus Christ" known both to Ignatius and the church at Magnesia? Unfortunately, there is not enough evidence available which could answer this question.

Between 95-150 A.D. a book of revelations, parables, and commands known as the Shepherd of Hermas was composed. Hermas might have been a brother of Pius, the bishop of Rome from 140-155 A.D.[8] The book was popular among the Christians in the second and third centuries because it stressed the importance of believers living pure lives. The Shepherd, who is the angel of repentance, showed Hermas ten allegorical visions. In one of them, Hermas saw a great willow tree which covered the plains and mountains. Underneath its shade stood all the people who called upon the name of the Lord. Hermas asked the Shepherd to interpret the vision. The Shepherd explained that the great tree "...is the law of God which was given to all the world. And this law is the Son of God, which is placed ...into the hearts of those who believe."[9] This is all that Hermas wrote on the Christian law of God. Again, whether this writing was calling attention to an actual teaching of the early church or was just using fanciful imagery in describing Jesus as law is uncertain.

The Letter of Barnabas is more specific in its comment on the New Law of Christ. This letter could

have been written as early as 71 A.D. or as late as
150 A.D. The unknown author of this letter believed
that the Old Testament prophets spoke on matters of
concern to the early Christian church. In his section
on sacrifices, the author cited an Old Testament
prophecy (Isaiah 1:11-13) which proved that God needed
neither sacrifices nor whole burnt offerings. These
offerings were set aside "...so that the new law of
our Lord Jesus Christ, which is not tied to a yoke of
necessity, might have its own offering which is not
man-made."[10] In this letter, the purpose of the New
Law of Christ is for the first time put into writing.
The New Law has replaced the old law, or the Mosaic
Law. Instead of burnt offerings, the Lord calls us to
approach with the offering made according to the New
Law. The sacrifice God desires to receive is a broken
spirit (Psalm 51:17).[11] This conviction that the
New Law of Christ supersedes the Mosaic Law frequently
appears in the Christian writings of the second
century A.D.

The Apologists

In the second century the Roman world recognized
that Christianity was a new faith rather than a sect
of Judaism. Other philosophic and religious systems
of that age began to view it as a threatening rival.
The Christians were often falsely accused of being
atheists, traitors, and even cannibals. To counter
these attacks, Christian apologists wrote "...to prove
and defend the superiority of the Christian
ethic."[12]

Probably, the first apology was the Preaching of
Peter of the early second century. It was a popular
work, though only fragments of it have survived.
These fragments can be found in several writings,
including the Stromata of Clement of Alexandria.
There is one reference in the Preaching of Peter
that connects Jesus with a law. Clement of Alexandria
reported that in that book Jesus is called both "Law
and Word."[13]

Sometimes the apologists used the literary form of
the dialogue. A famous writer who employed this
literary device was Justin Martyr (c. 110-165 A.D.).
A Gentile born in Palestine, he traveled around the
Mediterranean world studying various
philosophies--Stoicism, Pythagoreanism, and Platonism.
In Ephesus he met an elderly Christian who told him
that Jesus had fulfilled the Messianic prophecies

foretold in the writings of the Hebrew prophets. This conversation was decisive in Justin's decision to become a Christian. Afterwards, Justin used his philosophical talents to become an important defender of the faith. He remained a faithful witness throughout his life, which ended c. 165 A.D. when he was beheaded in Rome for being a Christian. Hence, the surname "Martyr" was appended to his given name in recognition of his faithfulness.

Justin's two most famous works are his First Apology (c. 150 A.D.) and the Dialogue with Trypho (c. 155-160 A.D.). The former work was addressed to the Emperor Antoninus Pius (138-161 A.D.) and was an answer to the charge against the Christians that they were atheists. The other work is reputedly a record of a discussion which Justin had with a Jew names Trypho. Justin tried to prove to Trypho that Jesus had fulfilled the Jewish Messianic prophecies and thus was the Christ. Besides contending with the Jews, it has been suggested that the purpose of the Dialogue with Trypho was to rebut the claims of Marcion (d.c. 160 A.D.), who taught that the God of the Hebrew prophets was not the same God of Jesus.

At the onset of the conversation, Trypho criticized the Christians for not keeping the Mosaic Law. Justin responded by stating that Christians trust in only one God, the God of Abraham, Isaac, and Jacob.

> But we do not trust through Moses or through the law, for then we would do the same as yourselves. But now--(for I have read that there shall be a final law, and a covenant the chiefest of all, which it is now incumbent on all men to observe, as many as are seeking after the inheritance of God. For the law promulgated on Horeb is now old, and belongs to yourselves alone, but this one is for all universally. Now law placed against law has abrogated that which is before it, and a covenant which comes after in like manner has put an end to the previous one; and an eternal and final law--namely Christ--has been given to us, and the covenant is trustworthy, after which there shall be no law, no commandment, no ordinance.[14]

Next, Justin quoted Isaiah 51:4-5, "...for a law shall go out from me," and Jeremiah 31:31, "Behold days are coming when I shall make a new covenant..."

to demonstrate that the Old Testament prophesied that a final law would come and abolish the Mosaic Law.[15]

The above quotations verify that Justin accepted the doctrine of the New Law of Christ. Just like the author of the Letter of Barnabas, Justin said the New Law was the Christian's theological justification for no longer observing the Mosaic Law. But unlike the Letter of Barnabas, Justin further expounds on how the New Law is different. It calls on Christians to stop fighting. For even if Christians suffer "...by wicked men and demons, so that even amid cruelties unutterable, death and torments, we pray for mercy to those who inflict such things upon us, and do not wish to give the least retort to anyone, even as the New Lawgiver has commanded us."[16]

Here is the first written link between the New Law and pacifism. It is significant that this link was found in the writings of the first Christian author who addressed the issue of Christians and participation in warfare. In his First Apology, Justin wrote:

> And when the Spirit of prophecy speaks as predicting things that are to come to pass, He speaks this way: 'For out of Zion shall go forth the law, and the word of the Lord from Jerusalem. And He shall judge among the nations, and shall rebuke many peoples; and they shall beat their swords into ploughshares, and their spears into pruning-hooks: nation shall not lift up sword against nation, neither shall they learn war anymore.' And that it did so come to pass, we can convince you. For from Jerusalem there went out into the world, men, twelve in number, and these illiterate, of no ability in speaking: but by the power of God they proclaimed to every race of men that they were sent by Christ to teach all the word of God; and we who formerly used to murder one another do not only refrain from making war upon our enemies; but also, that we may not lie nor deceive our examiners, willingly die confessing Christ.[17]

Justin believed that the coming of the New Law of Christ, which teaches all men to cease participating in warfare, was foretold in the prophecies of Isaiah (Isaiah 2:3-4). As it will be seen, this conviction continued in the writings against the heresies.

The Anti-heretical Writers
of the Late Second Century A.D.

Near the end of the second century A.D., the
Orthodox Christians were beset by the large number of
schismatic and heretical movements. The church's
three great rivals were the Marcionites, the Gnostics,
and the Manichaeans. To counter the threat of these
groups, Christian leaders launched an intense literary
campaign against these heresies.[18]   Of these
leaders, Irenaeus (c. 120-c. 202 A.D.) ranks as the
heretics' most formidable foe.

Originally from Asia Minor, Irenaeus arrived in
western Europe as a missionary to southern Gaul. In
177 A.D., after a period of persecution, Irenaeus
succeeded the martyred Pothinus as bishop of Lugdunum
(modern Lyon, France). It was after this time that
Irenaeus wrote his famous treatise Against Heresies
(c. 180 A.D.).

Against Heresies was written to refute the
teachings of the Gnostics and of the Marcionites. In
this defense of the Christian faith, he showed that he
was familiar with the teaching of the New Law. For
instance, in the fourth book of this treatise,
Irenaeus rebutted the Marcionite claim that the New
Covenant prophesied by Jeremiah (Jeremiah 31:31) had
begun with Zerubbabel's rebuilding of the Jerusalem
temple in the sixth century B.C. Irenaeus answered
that the Jews

...used the Mosaic law until the coming of
the Lord; but from the Lord's advent, the New
covenant which brings back peace, and the law
which gives life, has gone forth over the
whole earth, as the prophets said: 'For out
of Zion shall go forth the law, and the word
of the Lord from Jerusalem; and He shall
rebuke many people; and they shall break
their swords into plough-shares, and their
spears into pruning-hooks, and they shall no
longer learn to fight.' If therefore another
law and word, going forth from Jerusalem,
brought in such a reign of peace among the
Gentiles which received it (the word), and
convinced, through them, many a nation of its
folly, then only it appears that the prophets
spake of some other person. But if the law
of liberty, that is, the word of God,
preached by the apostles (who went forth from

Jerusalem) throughout all the earth, caused
such a change in the state of things, that
these nations did form the swords and
war-lances into ploughshares, and changed
them into pruning-hooks for reaping the corn,
that is, into instruments used for peaceful
purposes, and that they are now unaccustomed
to fighting, but when smitten offer also the
other cheek, then the prophets have not
spoken these things of any other person, but
of Him, who effected them. This person is
our Lord.[19]

Most assuredly, "the law which gives life" and "the
law of liberty" of which Irenaeus spoke in the above
passage referred to the New Law of Christ. In
addition, Irenaeus stated that he believed that the
proclamation of this New Law with the word of the
gospel was predicted by the prophet Isaiah (Isaiah
2:3-4), and explains why Christians will not fight.

Another western anti-heretical writer who believed
Jesus and his disciples fulfilled the prophecy of
Isaiah 2:3-4 was Tertullian of Carthage (c. 160-c. 220
A.D.). A prolific author, Tertullian wrote many
apologies, polemics, and instructional tracts. His
two most famous polemics are Against the Jews and
Against Marcion. Both works identified the law
having gone forth from Jerusalem as the New Law of
Christ.

In Against the Jews Tertullian wrote,
...and in another place he says, 'Behold,
days shall come, saith the Lord, and I will
draw up for the house of Judah and the house
of Jacob, a new testament; not such as I once
gave their fathers in the day wherein I led
them out from the land of Egypt.' Whence we
understand that the coming cessation of the
former circumcision then given, and the
coming procession of a new law (not such as
he had already given to the fathers), are
announced: just as Isaiah foretold... 'For
from Zion shall go out a law, and the word of
the Lord out of Jerusalem...'[20]

Tertullian agreed that this New Law instructs
Christians not to participate in warfare:
"Who else therefore are understood but we,
who, fully taught by the new law, observe
these practices, the old law being
obliterated, the coming of whose abolition
the action itself demonstrates? For the wont

of the old law was to avenge itself by the
vengeance of the glaive, and to pluck out
'eye for eye,' and to inflict retaliatory
revenge for injury. But the new law's wont
was to point to clemency, and to convert to
tranquility the pristine ferocity of
'glaives' and 'lances' and to remodel the
pristine execution of 'war' upon the rivals
and foes of the law into the pacific actions
of 'ploughing' and tilling the land...the
observance of the new law and the spiritual
circumcision has shown out into the voluntary
obedience of peace.[21]

Tertullian's conviction that Jesus brought a New
Law was so firm that he included it within his rule of
faith, a creedal statement to be used by the churches.
This rule of faith is found in his book On
Prescription Against Heretics. Of Jesus he
confessed,

...this Word is called His Son...was made
flesh in her womb, and, being born of her,
went forth as Jesus Christ; thenceforth He
preached the new law and the new promise of
the Kingdom of heaven, worked miracles,
having been crucified He arose again the
third day,...[22]

A contemporary of Irenaeus and Tertullian was
Archelaus (c. 277 A.D.), a bishop of Mesopotamia. The
book The Acts of the Disputation with the Heresiarch
Manes records how several times Archelaus debated
with Manes, the founder of the Manichaean religion (to
which Augustine belonged before he converted to
Orthodox Christianity). Manes taught that the Law of
Moses was contrary to the teachings of Jesus and did
not issue forth from the same God. Archelaus, in
denying this, tried to prove that the '...whole Old
Testament agrees with the New Testament, and is in
perfect harmony with the same."[23]

In the disputation, as Archelaus explained Manes'
doctrinal position, he repeatedly referred to the
teachings of Jesus as the New Law.

This man then maintained that the law of
Moses, to speak shortly, does not proceed
from the good God, but from the prince of
evil; and that it has no kinship with the new
law of Christ, but is contrary and hostile to
it...I understand then, that his chief effort
was directed to prove that the law of Moses
was not consonant with the law of Christ.[24]

In the anti-heretical writers, it is evident that the teaching of the New Law of Christ was widely accepted. In addition, its link with Christian pacifism was strengthened with the belief that Isaiah 2:3-4 foretold of the spread of the New Law of Christ and of its effect in changing belligerent hearts into peaceful souls. This harkening back to the Old Testament text to establish the biblical soundness of the New Law teaching may have several origins.

First of all, among the Jews there was a teaching that the Messiah would announce a New Torah.[25] Perhaps the church, when it was still predominantly Jewish, adopted this belief and began to search for scriptural references to support this view.

Another theory is that the early Christians, possibly even before the Gospels were written, compiled various Old Testament passages into a booklet.[26]   The purpose of these booklets, sometimes referred to as testimonies, was "...to convince the Jews out of the Old Testament itself that the Old Law was abolished, that its abolition was foreseen in the Old Testament, and that its purpose had been to prepare and prefigure the New Law of Christ."[27]

A third possibility was that the Christian writers of this period were interpreting the Old Testament in a typological manner. Sometimes the future Messianic Kingdom was described as a New Paradise, a New Flood, or a New Exodus.[28]   By perceiving the coming kingdom as a New Exodus, Jesus would be seen as a New Moses who leads his people out of a worldly Egypt into spiritual freedom. And the Sermon on the Mount would be regarded as the New Law given to the church by the New Lawgiver.[29]   Whatever this teaching's origin is, it will be seen that many writers of the third century A.D., notably from North Africa, affirmed the belief that Isaiah 2:3-4 spoke of the New Law of Christ.

The Church Fathers of the Third Century A.D.

By the third century A.D., the Christian Catechetical school of Alexandria was producing some of early Christianity's finest scholars. The first recorded president of the school was Pantaenus. This is known by the writings of Clement of Alexandria (c. 150-220 A.D.), his student.

Clement of Alexandria taught at the school of Alexandria from about 190-202 A.D., doing most of his writing at this time. His extant works include the Stromata or Miscellanies, The Instructor, and

An Exhortation to the Heathen. Although Clement did
not write on the topic of the New Law, he seems to
have agreed with several key points of this doctrine.
In his Exhortation to the Heathen, he rebuked the
pagans for trusting in myths and for not looking
upward to Zion for salvation:

> For out of Zion shall go forth the law, and
> the word of the Lord from Jerusalem--the
> celestial Word, the true athlete crowned in
> the theater of the whole universe.[30]

In other works, he wrote his readers to consider
Jesus as "King and Parent, who is truly law,"[31] and
to "...regard the Word as law."[32]

Another teacher at the school of Alexandria was
Origen (c. 185-254 A.D.), one of early Christianity's
greatest scholars and writers. A native of
Alexandria, he was a member of the Alexandrian Church
until 230 A.D., when he had a falling out with
Demetrius, the bishop of Alexandria. So Origen moved
to Caesarea, where he continued to teach and write.
It was in Caesarea that Origen wrote his apologetic
work Against Celsus (c. 245 A.D.).

Against Celsus was Origen's answer to the charges
made against the Christians by the pagan author Celsus
(c. 185 A.D.). Celsus' work is not extant, but much
of it can be recovered from Origen's book since he
responded to Celsus' accusations point by point.
Celsus, like Trypho, had criticized the Christians for
abandoning the ancestral customs and laws of the Jews.
Origen maintained that the Christian traditions had
emanated from the same source as the Jewish law had.
For evidence, Origen pointed back to the prophecy of
Isaiah 2:3:

> For the law came forth from the dwellers of
> Zion, and settled among us as a spiritual
> law. Moreover, the word of the law came
> forth from that very Jerusalem, that it might
> be disseminated through all places...And to
> those who inquire of us whence we come, or
> who is our founder, we reply that we are
> come, agreeably to the counsels of Jesus, to
> cut down our hostile and insolent wordy
> swords into ploughshares, and to convert into
> pruning-hooks the spears formerly employed in
> war. For we no longer take up sword against
> nation, nor do we learn war anymore, having
> become children of peace, for the sake of
> Jesus, who is our leader...and having

received a law, for which we give thanks to
Him.[33]

In another passage Origen defended the Christians
whom Celsus had said had revolted against the Jewish
state, as (he thought) the Jews violently rebelled
against the Egyptians under the leadership of Moses.
Origen denied that this took place and stated that,

...neither Celsus nor they who think with him
are able to point out any act on the part of
the Christians which savors of rebellion.
And yet, if a revolt had led to a formation
of the Christian commonwealth, so that it
derived its existence in this way from that
of the Jews, who were permitted to take up
arms in defense of the members of their
families and to slay their enemies, the
Christians' Lawgiver would not have
altogether forbidden the putting of men to
death; and yet He nowhere teaches that it is
right for his disciples to offer violence to
anyone, however wicked. For he did not deem
it in keeping with such laws as His, which
were derived from a divine source, to allow
the killing of any individual whatever. Nor
would the Christians, had they owed their
origin to a rebellion, have adopted laws of
so exceedingly mild a character as not to
allow them, when it was their fate to be
slain as sheep, upon any occasion to resist
their persecutors.[34]

This passage competently demonstrates how the New Law
contrasted with the Mosaic Law in that it prohibits
Christians from killing anyone, even in self-defense.
Origen went even one step further in his defense by
arguing that God fights to deliver them.

But with regard to the Christians, because
they were taught not to avenge themselves
upon their enemies (and thus observed laws of
a mild and philanthropic character); and
because they would not, although able, have
made war even if they had received authority
to do so, they have obtained this reward from
God, that he has always warred in their
behalf,...not permitting the whole nation to
be exterminated, but that the whole world
should be filled with their salutary and
religious doctrine.[35]

Another African leader who wrote on the New Law was
Cyprian, the bishop of Carthage (c. 210-258 A.D.). In

his Testimonies Against the Jews, he argued that the
misfortune of the Jews (the loss of Jerusalem and the
temple) was foretold in the prophetical writings, as
was the cessation of the Mosaic Law. Points 9 and 10
of his first book deal with this subject:

> 9. That the former law which was given by
> Moses was to cease.
> In Isaiah: "Then shall they be manifest who
> seal the law, that they may not learn, and he
> shall say, 'I wait upon the Lord, who turneth
> away His face from the house of Jacob, and I
> shall trust in Him.'" In the Gospel also:
> "All the prophets and the law prophesied
> until John."
> 10. That a New Law was to be given.
> To Micah: "For the law shall go forth out of
> Zion, and the word of the Lord from
> Jerusalem. And He shall judge among many
> peoples, and He shall subdue and uncover
> strong nations." Likewise in the Gospel
> according to Matthew: "And behold a voice
> out of the cloud saying, 'This is my beloved
> Son in whom I am well pleased; hear ye
> Him.'"[36]

A different perspective on the New Law is found in
the theology of the Latin writer Commodianus, a North
African bishop. The traditionally accepted date for
his writings is c. 250 A.D., but some scholars think
he may have lived in the fourth or fifth centuries
A.D. His two works, both poems, are the Carmen
Apology and the Instructions.

In the Instructions, Commodianus compares the two
trees of paradise—the tree of knowledge of good and
evil and the tree of life—and their fruit.

> Adam was the first who fell, and...the tree
> of the apple being tasted, death entered the
> world. By this tree of death we are born to
> the life to come. On the tree depends the
> life that bears fruit-precepts. Now
> therefore, pluck believingly the fruits of
> life. A law was given from the tree to be
> feared by the primitive man, whence comes
> death by the neglect of the law of the
> beginning. Now stretch forth your hand, and
> take of the tree of life. The excellent law
> of the Lord which follows has issued from the
> tree...If you wish to live, surrender
> yourself to the second law.[37]

According to Commodianus' theology, all humans have
the same choice to make as Adam did. We can either
pick of the fruit of the tree of knowledge of good and
evil or we can choose to eat of the fruit of the tree
of life. The one choice would mean living under the
Law of Moses and awaiting death. The other, that one
would live under the Law of Christ, and live. In his
poem, Commodianus is less interested in contrasting
the precepts of these two laws than in showing how
they are to be implemented into one's life, one by
works, the second by faith.

Though Commodianus did not seem concerned with what
the second law had to say about Christians'
participation in warfare, a writing from a fellow
African writer of the fourth century A.D. shows that
others continued to acknowledge the connection between
Christ's Law and pacifism.

The Early Fourth Century A.D. Writers

In the first quarter of the fourth century A.D.,
two Latin writers stand out, Arnobius (d.c. 330 A.D.)
and his pupil Lactantius (c. 250-c. 320 A.D.).
Arnobius was a teacher of rhetoric and oratory in
Sicca, North Africa. For a long time he spoke against
Christianity. When he converted to the Christian
faith (c. 300 A.D.), the local bishop insisted that he
first prove that his repentance was sincere before he
would be allowed to join the church. Therefore,
Arnobius published his Against the Heathen (c.
304-311 A.D.).

In this polemic, Arnobius wrote a defense against
the charge leveled at the Christians that since the
time they began proclaiming their religion, the number
of wars had increased throughout the world. His
answer was that it seemed to him that the number of
wars had in fact decreased because more people were
becoming Christians.

> For since we, a numerous band of men as we
> are, have learned from His teachings and His
> laws that evil ought not to be requited with
> evil, that we should rather shed our own
> blood than stain our hands and our conscience
> with that of another, an ungrateful world is
> now for a long period enjoying a benefit from
> Christ, in as much as by His means the rage
> of savage ferocity has been softened, and has
> begun to withhold hostile hands from the
> blood of a fellow creature.[38]

At the same time Arnobius was writing Against the Heathen, his student Lactantius was writing his principle work, the Divine Institutes (c. 304-311 A.D.). Lactantius' purpose for writing this book was to prove the errors of the pagan religion and to give a defense of the Christian faith. In one response where he explained why Christians did not observe the Mosaic Law, Lactantius demonstrated that he acknowledged the doctrine of the New Law of Christ. He answered that Jesus did not terminate the use of the Mosaic Law by His own will, but that this was done,

...in accordance to the will of God and after the predictions of the prophets. For Micah announced that He would give a new law in these terms, "The law shall go forth of Zion, and the word of the Lord from Jerusalem. And he shall judge among many people, and rebuke strong nations." For the former law, which was given by Moses, was not given on Mount Zion, but on Mount Horeb; and the Sibyl shows that it would come to pass that this law would be destroyed by the Son of God.[39]

Lactantius believed that Moses himself had foreseen the day a New Law would abolish the law handed down to him. For the Lord told Moses that there would someday be sent

..."a prophet from among their brethren like unto thee;" ...The Lord evidently announced by the law-giver himself that He was about to send His own Son—that is, a law alive, and present in person, and destroy that old law given by a mortal, that by Him who was eternal He might ratify afresh a law which was eternal.[40]

To confirm this prophecy, Moses began calling his successor, Hoshea son of Nun, Joshua or Jesus "...to show that the new law was about to succeed to the old law which was given by Moses."[41]

The writings of Arnobius and Lactantius give evidence that while Christianity was still an outlawed religion, its defenders employed the doctrine of the New Law of Christ in their answers to its critics. But after the issuance of the so-called Edict of Milan in 313 A.D., the usage of this doctrine in Christian writings waned.

There are several possibilities to explain the decline of the teaching of the New Law in later Christian writings. 1) Christianity became one of

Rome's legal religions in 313 A.D. and the empire'e official religion by 391 A.D. This change in its relationship to the state could have altered the church's position on Christian participation in the military. As a result, the appeal to the pacifistic New Law by Christian writers also declined. 2) In its attempt to discredit the heretical claims that the teachings of Jesus were contradictory to the commandments of the Mosaic Law, the church may have over-emphasized the harmony of the Old Testament with the New Testament, thereby abandoning the claim that Jesus brought a New Law. 3) Church canon law, developing from the many councils held after Christianity became a legal religion, could have replaced the teaching of the New Law. 4) The church became preoccupied with combatting new threats to the faith. The heresy of Arianism overshadowed the earlier heresies of Marcionism and Gnosticism. From the time of the Nicene Council (325 A.D.), the church writers were more involved with debates over various Christological theories than in explaining why Christianity did not keep the Mosaic Law.

Conclusion

The purpose of this paper has been to establish that the Christian church of the first three centuries A.D. proclaimed that Jesus delivered a New Law which superseded the Mosaic Law. The evidence was traced back to some of Christianity's earliest writings and was found in the works of many, including the church's best known authors. By the third century A.D., this teaching appears to have been widely disseminated throughout the whole Roman world, from Gaul to North Africa, from Rome to Mesopotamia.

It has been seen that the early Christian writers pointed back to the Old Testament prophecies, especially to Isaiah 2:3-4, when they defended the scriptural validity of the New Law of Christ. They believed that the first apostles went out from Jerusalem with this law and with the word of the gospel. The result of their work was that many accepted the Christian faith and as a consequence refrained from participating in warfare and the military.

While this belief in the apostles fulfilling the prophecy of Isaiah 2:3-4 can be found in Christian writings predating the so-called Edict of Milan of 313 A.D., very little mention of the New Law of Christ is

made after this period. I have suggested several
reasons for this topic's decline in the church's
writings. Yet one should not think that this teaching
disappeared altogether.

One piece of evidence that demonstrates that
knowledge of the New Law of Christ continued after the
early half of the fourth century A.D. can be found in
early Christian art. An important theme in Christian
art of the second century to sixth century A.D. was
the "Traditio Legis" or "Christ giving the Law."
Frequently this art theme decorated the apse of
basilicas.[42]

A mosaic of this theme can be found in the
mausoleum of Constanza, the daughter of Emperor
Constantine (324-337 A.D.). The mosaic, dated c. 350
A.D., depicts Jesus standing upon Mt. Zion handing
down a scroll to St. Peter, who stands to Jesus' left.
At Christ's right side is St. Paul who lifts his hand
in adoration of the Lord. At the feet of these three
figures are four sheep, representing the flock of the
church.

Often in this theme of "Christ giving the Law," the
scroll which Jesus presents to St. Peter has the
inscription "Dominus legem dat" upon it. This phrase
means "the Lord gives the law." So the scroll
represents the law handed down to the church.[43]

What is the origin of this theme? Other Christian
art themes, such as "Christ giving the keys" to St.
Peter, can be traced back to the New Testament. But
the New Testament does not describe the event of
Christ giving a New Law to the apostles. The most
probable explanation for this theme's origin is the
early Christians' writings of the New Law of Christ.
In these writings, the depictions of Jesus giving a
New Law to the apostles, who are represented in this
art work by St. Peter and St. Paul, seem very vivid.

Further testimony to show knowledge and acceptance
of the doctrine of the New Law of Christ may be found
in the statements of two Christian saints who refused
to join or remain in the Roman legions because their
faith forbid them to do so. During the reign of the
Roman Emperor Diocletian (285-305 A.D.) an order was
proclaimed that the sons of his soldiers must also
become soldiers. One veteran brought his son,
Maximilian, to be enlisted into the army. Maximilian
protested and declared, "I am not allowed (licet) to
be a soldier, for I am a Christian."[44] His refusal
led to his execution on that same day in 295 A.D.

St. Martin of Tours (c. 315-395 A.D.), a son of a
veteran, was already in the army when he converted to
Christianity. Some time after that, the day before
his legion was to take part in a battle, Martin asked
his superior officer for a discharge. He said,

> Hitherto I have served you as a soldier.
> Allow me now to become a soldier of God. Let
> the man who is to serve you receive your
> donative. I am a soldier of Christ. It is
> not lawful (licet) for me to fight.[45]

At first his request was denied. But unexpectedly on the
next day the enemy surrendered before the battle began
and Martin was given permission to leave.

Jean-Michel Hornus translated the two above
quotations from Latin in his book It Is Not Lawful
For Me To Fight. In one quote he translated the verb
licet to mean "allowed," in another to mean
"lawful." Both translations are correct. But if one
could assume that in their statements, Maximilian and
Martin were using licit to specifically express the
meaning "lawful," then it is possible that both
Maximilian and St. Martin were referring to the
doctrine of the New Law of Christ. Though the date of
St. Martin's dismissal from the Roman military is
uncertain, it is well after the year 313 A.D.

Additional data which shows an awareness of this
doctrine can be found in the study of certain medieval
sects, especially those which were concerned with the
church-state issue and were often pacifistic in their
teachings. Geoffrey Nuttall's Christian Pacifism in
History has a chapter entitled "The Law of Christ."
In it he reports that Wycliffe, the Lollards, the
Waldensians, and the Czech Brethren made mention of
the Law of Christ. In fact, the fifteenth century
Czech Brethren's official name was "The Brethren of
the Law of Christ."[46]

What significance this doctrine had on the
pacifistic Anabaptists will have to be discovered in
another study. But it is known that Hans Denck, an
Anabaptist theologian and a writer (c. 1495-1527), was
aware of it. In his book Concerning Genuine Love he
wrote,

> From all this it becomes clear now that there
> is no more than one Love in the old and new
> Law (as it is called), except of course in
> the new Law this Love has been made known and
> shown to the people of God through Jesus his
> helper.[47]

Thus, in practice, if not necessarily in the same words, the legacy of the doctrine of the New Law of Christ has remained within the Christian church through the witness of those Christians who, because of the gospel of Jesus, have refused to take part in warfare and the military.

1. Frederick H. Russell, The Just War in the Middle Ages, Cambridge Studies in Medieval Life and Thought, vol. 8 (Cambridge: Cambridge University Press, 1975; reprint ed., 1979), p. 10.

2. Two representative works on this subject are recommended. For an example of an article arguing that the early Christians were opposed to idolatry and not military service per se, read Edward A. Ryan, "The Rejection of Military Service by the Early Christians," Theological Studies 13 (March 1952): 1-32. A work that takes the opposite position is Jean-Michel Hornus, It Is Not Lawful For Me To Fight (Scottdale, Penn.: Herald Press, 1980).

3. Paul C. Finney, "Antecedents of Byzantine Iconoclasm: Christian Evidence Before Constantine" in The Image and the Word: Confrontations in Judaism, Christianity and Islam, ed. Joseph Gutmann, Society of Biblical Literature: Religion and the Arts, no. 4 (Missoula, Montana: Scholars Press, 1977), p. 34.

4. Edgar J. Goodspeed and Robert M. Grant, A History of Early Christian Literature (Chicago: University of Chicago Press, 1966), p. 7.

5. Ignatius, Magnesians 3.1, in The Apostolic Fathers, ed. Jack Sparks, (Nashville: Thomas Nelson Publishers, 1978), p. 87. (Henceforth abbrev. AF).

6. Ibid., 2.1, AF:86.

7. Ignatius, Ephesians 12, AF:81.

8. Goodspeed and Grant, A History of Early Christian Literature, p. 31.

9. Hermas, Similitudes 8.3.2-3, AF:225.

10. Letter of Barnabas 2.6, AF:270.

11. Ibid., 2.10, AF:270.

12. Jaroslav Pelikan, The Christian Tradition, vol. 1:   The Emergence of the Catholic Tradition (100-600) (Chicago: University of Chicago Press, 1971), p. 38.

3. Clement of Alexandria, Stromata 1:29 in James Donaldson and Alexander Roberts, eds. The Ante-Nicene Fathers, vol. 2 (Edinburgh 1977; reprint ed., Grand Rapids, Michigan: Wm. B. Eerdmans Publishing Company, 1977), p. 341. (Henceforth abbrev. ANF).

14. Justin Martyr, Dialogue with Trypho 11, ANF vol. 1:199-200.

15. Ibid., ANF 1:200.

16. Ibid., ANF 1:203.

17. Justin Martyr, First Apology 39, ANF 1:175-76.

18. Goodspeed and Grant, A History of Early Christian Literature, p. 119.

19. Irenaeus, Against Heresies 4.34.4, ANF 1:512.

28. Tertullian, Against the Jews 3, ANF 3:154. See also Against Marcion 3, ANF 3:339.

21. Tertullian, Against the Jews 3, ANF 3:154.

22. Tertullian, On Prescription Against Heretics 13, ANF 3:249.

23. Archelaus, Disputation with the Heresiarch Manes 41, ANF 6:215.

24. Ibid., ANF 6:214-15.

25. Alfred Edersheim, The Life and Times of Jesus the Messiah (Grand Rapids, Michigan: Wm. B. Eerdmans Publishing Co., 1976), pp. 764-66.

26. Pelikan, The Christian Tradition 1, p. 16.

27. Irenaeus, Proof of the Apostolic Preaching, trans. and annot. Joseph P. Smith, Ancient Christian Writers, no. 16 (Westminster, Maryland: The Newman Press, 1952), p. 31.

28. Jean Danielou, From Shadow to Reality, trans. Wulstan Hibberd (London: Burns and Oates, 1960), p. 287.

29. Ibid., p. 159.

30. Clement of Alexandria, Exhortation to the Heathen 1, ANF 2:171.

31. Clement of Alexandria, Stromata 7.3, ANF 2:527.

32. Clement of Alexandria, The Instructor 1.3, ANF 2:211.

33. Origen, Against Celsus 5.33, ANF 4:558.

34. Ibid., 3.7, ANF 4:467.

35. Ibid., 3.8, ANF 4:467-68.

36. Cyprian, Testimonies Against the Jews 1.9-10, ANF 5:510.

37. Commodianus, Instructions 35, ANF 4:209-10.

38. Arnobius, Against the Heathen 1.6, ANF 6:415.

39. Lactantius, Divine Institutes 4:17, ANF 7:118.

40. Ibid.

41. Ibid., ANF 7:119.

42. The New Encyclopaedia Britannica: Micropaedia, 15th ed., s.v. "Christ Giving the Law."

43. More information on the term "Traditio Legis" can be found in the following reference work: Gertrud Schiller, Ikonographie der Christlichen Kunst, 4 vols. (Gutersloh, Germany: Gutersloher Verlagshaus Gerd Mohn, 1966), Bard 3:202-216.

44. Hornus, It is not Lawful for Me to Fight, p. 133.

45. Ibid., p. 144.

46. Geoffrey Nuttall, Christian Pacifism in History (Berkeley, California: A World Without War Publications, 1977), p. 26.

47. Hans Denck, Selected Writings of Hans Denck, ed. and trans. Edward J. Furcha, Pittsburgh Original Texts and Translations Series, no. 1 (Pittsburgh: The Pickwick Press, 1975), p. 108.

WAR AND PEACE IN THE PATRISTIC AGE

JOHN FRIESEN

The patristic age is germinal[1] for much of the subsequent history of the church.[1] It is the age which gradually evolved a canon which it felt expressed its life and faith in Jesus Christ. It is the age which faced the task of translating the gospel from one culture to another and then of providing terminology and concepts which would adequately communicate the gospel within the newly adopted culture. The conclusions which the church arrived at, often haltingly, seldom unanimously, have exercised surprising influence upon the subsequent history of the church.

One important issue which the patristic church faced was that of peace and war. All sources indicate that during the first two centuries the church was pacifist, both in theology and practise.[2] It interpreted pacifism to mean rejection of violence including use of the sword. It is equally clear that at the end of the patristic age the church had radically changed its stand on pacifism. Not only had the church accepted the use of the sword, but it had also articulated a theological basis for the use of the sword. Why did this shift occur? This study will attempt to clarify the nature of the shift and some of the reasons why it happened.

I. A PACIFIST CHURCH BORN OF A HEBREW FATHER, AND GREEK AND LATIN MOTHERS.

Jesus was a Jew born in Judaea and raised in Galilee. His disciples were from Judaea and Galilee. The first churches were composed largely of Jews and hearers at the synagogues. The earliest Christian writings were the letters of Paul, and the parables and sayings of Jesus handed on orally from person to

person. The gospel of Jesus was conveyed within the
Jewish culture, language, and thought patterns.

The early church's Jewish character created some
problems for it. The Roman empire had given a number
of religions the legal right to exist within its
borders. Judaism had this right. Yet it was a
precarious right, for the Romans viewed the Jews as
giving grudging allegiance to the empire. Thus for
Jews the possibility for persecution was constantly
present. As the Christian church grew and was
persecuted by an empire which saw it as an unpatriotic
sect, the Jews attempted to dissociate themselves from
Christianity. Some of the early persecutions against
Christians thus seem to have been inspired by the
Jews.

This caused the church to turn against Judaism.
But the church had a more significant reason for
attempting to dissociate itself from Judaism. As long
as the church was known as a sect of Judaism, maybe
after the order of Qumran, the scope of its expansion
was very limited. It could hardly hope to win any
significant number of Greeks, Romans and Persians. In
order to become a universal church, it needed to
escape the confines of Jewish sectarian particularity.

The second century witnessed various attempts to
conceptualize the Christian gospel in non-Jewish form.
Marcion attempted to develop a Christian canon which
would discard the old canon of the Septuagint, and
form a new canon composed of Christian writings which
showed little Jewish influence. His canon consisted
of the letters of Paul and the Gospel of Luke without
its first two chapters. The church rejected Marcion's
option as destroying something basic to the gospel.
The church was convinced that the Christian canon had
to include the Jewish canon.

Greeks were offended with the Christian confession
that in Christ God become human and took a material
body. They said Jesus must have had a spiritual body.
Ignatius, a Christian bishop, opposed this adamantly,
arguing that if Christ did not come in the flesh then
salvation was not accomplished in Christ. Basilides
and Valentinus, two Christian gnostics, formulated a
totally new cosmology which explained the salvation
story in non-Hebraic categories. Instead of heaven
there was a pleroma. Instead of creation there was
the falling out of the pleroma. Instead of the God of
Abraham, Isaac and Jacob there was the One, always

silent, unchangeable, unknowable, the source of all
Being. Instead of the salvation history from Abraham
to Jesus, there was a cosmic drama according to which
matter was formed from the passion of Sophia. Yahweh,
the God of Israel, was the father of Jesus, who
mistakenly thought he was the creator of the universe.

Irenaeus, a late second century bishop in Lyons,
articulated the church's rejection of the gnostic
re-reading of the salvation story. As a Greek, he
knew that Christianity had to be articulated in
non-Hebraic categories to be understandable to a wider
world. Rather than cosmological categories, he chose
historical categories, expressing the salvation story
as a historical process in which the second Adam,
Christ, recapitulated the promises of the first Adam,
and made a new start for humanity. Instead of basing
Christian faith and life on secret knowledge, he based
it on the three pillars of; the faithful leaders
(bishops) in the churches, the "regula fidei" or
"synopses" of faith which the various churches had
articulated, and the writings of the apostles.[4]

As the church attracted more and more Greeks, the
need to articulate the gospel in Greek categories
became more acute. One of the most influential
attempts was made by Origen, who was a Christian
teacher from 202-254, first at Alexandria and later at
Caesarea. In contrast to the cosmologies of the
Christian gnostics, Origen articulated a Christian
theology within the ontological categoreis of middle
Platonism. For him all Being emanated from, and
returned to, the source "arche" of all Being.[5] Even
though novel, Origen's theology was more sober than
that of the gnostics, and was designed to undercut
gnosticism in Alexandria. He based his theology on
both the, Septuagint and a selection of Christian
writings.

In the course of his work as a teacher, Origen was
asked to reply to Celsus, a Greek who had written a
very systematic, well reasoned document against
Christianity. He answered the charges by Celsus in a[6]
lengthy book entitled Contra Celsum in Latin.

Celsus accused Christians of irresponsibility
since they refused to hold public office, fight in the
army, and swear the oaths of allegiance to the state.
Celsus presented the Christians with the logical
alternative; they should either shoulder their civic
responsibility or opt out of life by not coming to
manhood, marrying wives, bringing up children, and

partaking of the blessings of life.[7] Origen rejected
the charge of irresponsibility. He replied that "he
truly discharges the duties of life who is ever
mindful who is his creater, and what things are
agreeable to Him, and who acts in all things so that
he may please God."[8]   Furthermore Origen said,
Christians do not act irresponsibly when they refuse
to bear the sword for the emperor. They support the
emperor through prayer which is more powerful than
armies.[9]

     If everyone did as Christians do, Celsus argued,
then the empire would be left defenseless. Origen
responded to this by saying that if the whole Roman
empire were to become pacifist as the Christians were,
it would not necessarily be overrun by the barbarians.
History he said, is not in human hands, but in God's,
and he would protect his own. Origen quoted Exodus
14:14 to indicate that God will protect his own and
that the believers are to be a people of peace, "The
Lord shall fight for you, and you shall hold your
peace."[10]   Celsus in his article argued that the
barbarians would not lay down their swords, but would
remain war-like. Origen responded that it was the
will of God that all, Romans and barbarians, would one
day lay down their swords as the Christians were now
already doing. For Origen, peace was the promise for
the future for all nations.[11]

     Celsus went on to accuse the Christians of failing
to support justice, otherwise they would "help the
king with all their might and labor with him in the
maintenance of justice, and fight for him." Origen
responded that the Christians do support justice. We
make "supplication, prayers, intercessions...for all
kings and for all that are in authority. (I Timothy
2:1,2).[12]   All who thus come to God in prayer ought to
be freed from the necessity to spill blood for that
would defile them in the sight of God. This, he says,
is even acknowledged by pagans in that they excuse
their priests from combat.[13]   It is noteworthy that he
claimed this privilege for all Christians, not simply
for clergy.

     Origen summed up his response to Celsus by saying
that "Christians are benefactors of their country more
than others. They train up citizens and inculcate
piety to the Supreme Being."[14]   If Christians do not
serve in civil offices it is because their first
responsibility is to the church and its mission to
bring people to God.

The western half of the Roman empire was Latin, even though much of the west was not even thoroughly Latinized. The Berbers in North Africa, Spaniards in Spain, and the various Gallic tribes maintained their culture in the face of the Roman conquerers. Irenaeus in Lyons complained that he had to speak mostly the local vulgar dialects. In North Africa the Berber-Roman conflict rent the church throughout the fourth and fifth century in what is known as the Donatist controversy.

The most sophisticated articulation of the Christian gospel in the west during the third century was by Tertullian, a Roman in North Africa. Tertullian was well educated, a lawyer by profession. He wrote and spoke a beautiful Latin, and even wrote a few treatises in Greek. As Origen set the basic direction for eastern theology, so Tertullian made a similar contribution to Latin theology.[15]

Tertullian was faced with a Christian gnosticism which he did his utmost to combat. In common with many in the early church he believed that gnosticism originatd in Greek philosophy. He concluded that philosophy was totally antithetical to Christianity. "What has Jerusalem to do with Athens?" he exclaimed.

Tertullian had a very strong sense of the role and place of the Christian community. He spent his life attempting to define it and guide it in the mission which he felt it ought to have. For him the Christian community was not a metaphysical entity about whose pre-existence one could speculate, nor an invisible union of all the elect, as in gnosticism. For him the church was an historical community of people who were fallible and weak, and who thus had to continually be on their quard against falling prey to the loyalties of the world. For him loyalty and faith in Christ, and the corollary rejection of the world, meant leaving the old life of immorality, expensive clothes, mythologies, and belief in the pantheon of gods, in exchange for a disciplined life which would give glory to God. His search for a disciplined, pure community led him to leave the large church and join the Montanists, and finally to found his own separate, pure, church.

In his treatise, <u>De Corona Militis</u>, Tertullian addressed the question of military service.[16] The occasion for writing was that one soldier, one of several Christians in the army, had refused to carry the laurel wreath when the troops were being given their booty after a battle. Because of his refusal the Christian soldier had been imprisoned and was now awaiting execution.

Tertullian indicated that he considered this soldier the only true Christian and the others who had worn the wreath as only nominal Christians. He said that the others had "rejected the prophecies of the Holy Spirit."[17] Tertullian opposed the wearing of the crown for a number of reasons. First, because the use of the crown was based purely on tradition and had no scriptural support.[18] Second, because it is contrary to nature for a person to wear a crown.[19] Third, the origin of wearing crowns lies in the mythological stories of the gods. In the Bible only Christ had a crown, and his became a crown of martyrdom, not a crown of military victory. So in wearing the victory crown, the Christian appears in the dress of an idol, of Belial.[20] Fourth, Terutllian said that a soldier denies Christ in that he has to swear the oath of loyalty (sacramentum) "to another master after Christ."[21] This seemed to be the heart of Terutllian's objection to military service, for he proceeded to ask a number of rhetorical questions.

"Shall it be held lawful to make an occupation of the sword when the Lord proclaims that he who uses the sword shall perish by the sword?" "And shall the son of peace take part in battle when it does not become him even to sue at law?" "And shall he keep guard before the temples which he has renounced?"[22]

Tertullian concluded his discussion by summarizing his objections to wearing the military crown, which he extended to rejection of all military service. First, wearing the crown is idolatry. "There is one gospel, and the same Jesus, who will one day deny everyone who denies him and acknowledge everyone who acknowledges God."[23] Second, by wearing the military crown the Christian refuses the one crown which the Christian can properly wear, namely the crown of martyrdom.[24] Third, to use the sword is to take the life of fellow believers for there are also Christians among barbarians.[25]

He counseled soldiers who had become Christians to leave military service, for otherwise "all sorts of quibbling will have to be resorted to in order to avoid offending God, and that is not even allowed outside of military service."[26]

The evidence indicates that up to 170 A.D. there

were probably no Christians in the Roman armies.
After 170 the inscriptions and the writings of the
fathers indicate that some Christians were serving in
the army.[27]   It is evident, though, that as the church
shifted from its Jewish base to both the Greek and
Latin cultures, it retained its pacifism. Both Origen
and Tertullian articulated a belief in non-violence
and rejection of military service, the former in the
face of challenges from a cultured pagan, and the
latter with the purpose of developing a disciplined
Christian community.

II. THE PACIFISM OF ALL BECOMES THE PACIFISM OF THE FEW.

The third century witnessed the rapid growth and
acculturation of Christianity.   The former small
minority became a much more numerous minority.   The
church formerly composed of the poor and the outcasts
now also won some who were educated and rich. As it
won the rich and the educated, it adopted increasingly
more of the values and the lifestyle of the
Greco-Roman world.

Despite this rapid growth and acculturation, the
third century churches continued a strong and almost
unanimous objection to killing and the bearing of
arms.   Both Lactantius and Arnobius, late third
century Christian writers, claimed that Christians did
not shed blood.[28]   Until the early fourth century all
the major Christian writers in both the east and west
witnessed against serving in the army.

However, contemporary with this is also the
evidence that in practise Christians were serving as
soldiers in the army. The Thundering Legion recruited
in Armenia contained some Christians.[29]   In Syria,
Abgar IX, the king of Edessa (A.D. 179-216) was
converted to Christianity in A.D. 202 and for the
remainder of his reign made Christianity the official
religion of Osrhoene.[30]   Paul of Samosata, in 278 A.D.
was the first Christian bishop to hold the post of
civil magistrate and to employ a bodyguard.[31]

In the west the evidence of Christians in the army
is equally strong. Tertullian's objection to military
service witnessed to the presence of Christians in the
army. Pre-Constantinian inscriptions from Bensancon,[32]
Phrygia and Rome mention Christian soldiers.[33]
Cyprian mentioned two soldier martyrs.[33]   When the
persecution broke out under Diocletian and Galerius in

303, the attempt was made to weed Christians out of
the army. Christians in the army were some of the
first to feel the brunt of the persecution.[34]
It may be possible to say that some areas of the
empire were more pacifist than others, for example,
the interior more than the northern and eastern
frontiers which were constantly endangered. But this
simply helps to point out the fact that already in the
third century some Christians were serving in the
army.
Why did it occur and why was it allowed when the
sources are unanimous that military service was
contrary to tradition and condemned by scripture?
Pacifists have sometimes argued that Christian
soldiers in the second and third centuries were
engaged in police functions. Even though this
argument has some validity, the distinction is not of
great significance because in both its role as police
and military, the Roman army could use force and take
life. Non-pacifist churches have generally asked the
question differently. They have asked, "Why was the
early church pacifist?" Catholic scholars have
attempted to bring the position of the early church
into line with the later Thomistic formulation, by
ascribing the pacifism to non-pacifist considerations.
The fathers are said to have objected to military
service because of the danger of idolatry in the army
or because of aversion to Rome, the persecutor. If
there was genuine pacifism it was due to heresy. This
position assumes that military service is ordinarily
normative for the church. Protestant non-pacifists
have frequently assigned eschatology as the reason for
the early Christian abstention from warfare. Because
much of the early church expected an imminent end to
the course of history, Christians were unwilling to
accept civil and military responsibilities. Since the
early second and third century eschatological emphases
are normally considered heretical, this position also
assumes that early Christian pacifism was an
aberration.[35]
This study asks the historical question, "Why did
the early church which was pacifist gradually allow
its men to serve in the army?" The answer does not
lie in any fine distinction between military and
police functions. Rather, it will be argued, the
answer lies in a gradually changing ecclesiology later
buttressed with a new theology.
The first and second century churches were small

and fairly highly disciplined. The shepherd of
Hermas, among others, indicated that the church
disciplined itself according to a rather strict norm.
It interpreted those Christian writings quite
literally which referred to the church as pure and
spotless. Other Christian selections were also
interpreted literally, for example, the selections in
the gospel of Matthew which viewed the church as
pacifist.[36]

However, as the church expanded in number and as
it won the educated and rich, gradual but persistent
change was perceptible. The question was raised
whether a person could be both rich and a Christian in
good standing. It seems that the church had at one
time said no, for around the year 200 A.D., Clement, a
teacher in Alexandria, reinterpreted the Biblical
sayings on money and poverty.[37] He argued that the
New Testament sayings by Jesus did not mean what they
literally seemed to say, namely that Christians ought
to give away their possessions. Rather, Jesus meant
that the Christian's attitude to his wealth ought to
be one of detachment. He ought to regard his wealth
as though he had or would be willing to give it up.
This interpretation allowed the wealthy to keep their
possessions in good conscience. This new interpretation raised opposition within the church for many felt
that the church was becoming too worldly and was
allowing new converts into church without requiring
that they leave the ways of the world.

Around 220 A.D. a controversy occurred in Rome
between two Christian factions over the issue whether
immorality ought to be disciplined severely.
Hippolytus argued that according to tradition
immorality was forbidden. If some Christian committed
adultery he or she should be disciplined, possibly
with excommunication. A much more liberal position
was taken by Pope Callistus, a former slave who had
been accused of stealing money. Hippolytus accused
Callistus of courting the favour of immoral people by
pronouncing that everyone could be forgiven.
He accused him also of destroying church discipline.
Earlier, those who lived in immorality had been
removed from the church; now the immoral were crowding
into Callistus' church.[38]

The two factions continued in Rome even after
Hippolytus and Callistus had died, with the more
lenient position gradually gaining the loyalty of the
majority of Roman Christians. A similar controversy

occurred in the 250s after the persecution by Decius.
The issue was how severely to deal with those who had
lapsed into apostasy during the persecution, and had
offered incense to the genius of the emperor.
Novatian was leader of the element in the Roman church
which argued that those who had publicly denied Christ
in the persecution while others had given up their
life could not simply be reaccepted as members in good
standing. Their sin had been so heinous that only God
in his infinite grace could forgive them. The church
could not reaccept them as members. They were to be
dealt with according to Matthew 10:33, "Whosoever
shall deny me before men, him shall I deny before my
Father who is in heaven."[39]

Others, led by the Pope, argued that God's
forgiveness was unlimited, and the church ought to
forgive those who had lapsed. Even priests who had
lapsed ought to be forgiven. They quoted Joel 2:13,
"Be ye converted to the Lord your God, for he is
merciful, and one who pities with great compassion."[40]

In the Syrian church in the East, it seems from
recently discovered papyri, that the ethical
requirements of full membership were very high.
Celibacy and pacifism may have been two of the
requirements of membership. This meant that there
were many Christians of lesser dedication and
practise, but they were not accorded full membership
in the church.[41]

There was a gradual relaxing of ethical standards
in the second and third centuries as the church
expanded. For many this change was a sign of the
church's growing maturity, especially in regards to
its view of salvation. Others, however, lamented this
trend and saw it as the betrayal of the traditional
interpretation of the gospel. They saw this
development as evidence of the church adopting the
ways of the world. At the end of the third century
there began a lay renewal movement, which started in
Egypt, and gradually spread throughout the East. The
renewal movement was in the form of monasticism, both
eremitic and cenobitic. Monasticism offered highly
dedicated men and women a life in which the Christian's dedication could be more consistently
expressed. Their disciplined life caught the
imagination of many Christians and thousands flocked
to the desert monks to be inspired, taught and healed
by them. By the mid fourth century at least eight
thousand people, men and women, lived a monastic life

in Egypt alone.[42]

By the end of the third century, the church saw itself as a community composed of varying degrees of dedication and performance. Some members were of high dedication who lived exemplary lives and resisted apostasy in the persecutions. Others, however, were of rather low dedication. It was also not true that the clergy could be identified as the former and the laity as the latter, since clergy apostasized in the persecutions under Decius and Diocletian, and the desert monks were lay members, who exemplified a high dedication and thus were critiquing the worldliness of the hierarchy of the church. The important point is that during the third century there was a noticeable change from the earlier view of the church as a communio sanctorum, a holy community, to the church as a schoolmaster who strives to meet the needs of the weakest as well as the most dedicated.

This development of an ecclesiology which allowed for greatly varying levels of dedication and performance provided the church with a hermeneutic by which it was able to accept military service and civil offices. The pacifist sections of the New Testment could continue to be taught, but the church did not expect that everyone would be able to live up to the peace emphasis. The church was willing to accept widely varying responses to its teachings. In this manner the church did not have to deny its own history nor the witness of the scriptures.

III. TRANSFORMATION OF THE CHURCH FROM A PERSECUTED MINORITY TO THE COHESIVE CEMENT OF THE EMPIRE.

The fourth century church underwent a very traumatic transformation. In the decade from 303 to 312 it passed from the most severe persecution in its history to being accepted by the son of a Caesar, Constantine, as the favored religion. The literature of the period indicates that the psychological impact of the transition from persecution to acceptance was so profound that it was difficult for the church carefully to sift out the issues involved in this momentous change.

In 312 when Constantine was attempting to gain victory over the other Augusti and Caesars, the Roman empire was in desperate shape. From 235 to 284 it had tottered from civil war to civil war, from assassination to assassination. Diocletian (284-305) had reorganized the empire into four sections and had provided for the orderly transfer of "imperium" from Augusti to Caesars. This system crashed into civil war almost immediately after Diocletian retired to the Danube in 305.[43]

Besides the political instability, the resources of the empire had been thoroughly squandered. The currency had been debased over and over again, the troops were of questionable loyalty, and the Germanic tribes were threatening the northern borders. What was obviously needed was some new vision which could inspire the kind of national mission among the people of the empire as Augustus Caesar had given Rome during the first century B.C. Diocletian and Galerius thought that what was needed was a new, united dedication to the ancient values of the Romans. Consequently they tried to stamp out the various new religions including Christianity, and the church suffered its worst, and also last, systematic empire wide persecution. But the church, despite the loss of leaders, books, church buildings and large numbers of apostates, remained strong and unbowed. The persecution finally had to cease because it was unsuccessful.

Thus when Constantine in 312 faced his chosen destiny of attempting to gather the empire under his sole rule, he was still faced with the question as to what could be used to unite the empire, east with west, north with south, and give it a new vision. He chose the Christian religion for that task.

Some of the reasons for choosing Christianity were obvious. It had members in all parts of the empire. It was most numerous in the east which was still under the control of his rival Licinius. It had a strong structure of metropolitans, bishops, deacons and priests. The church had considerable internal discipline as the persecutions had shown. It seemed that the church was well suited to become the cohesive cement for a rejuvenated empire.[44]

During the night before the battle at the Milvian bridge, when in a dream Constantine saw the words written over the labarum "hoc signo vince," he saw this as divine blessing for the union of his projected united empire with the one united church. When he discovered that his chosen instrument, the church, was rent by controversy in North Africa, he promptly convened a council, pronounced judgement, and exiled bishops. That the unity of the church could not be

established by imperial decree was a major
disappointment to him. In 324, when Constantine
finally united the whole empire under his rule by
defeating Licinius, he was greatly annoyed to discover
a division within the eastern church--a division over
such a minor issue as whether the Son, Jesus Christ,
was like or the same as the Father. He quickly
arranged for a council at Nicaea in 325 over which he
presided, in which a creed was adopted which all
except two minor Egyptian bishops accepted. Now
finally both church and state were whole and could
together build a new and glorious future. One God,
one empire, one emperor, and one church seemed to be a
formula designed to assure greatness to Rome and to
Constantine. In self-congratulatory admiration of
his own accomplishments, he declared himself the
thirteenth apostle and founded an apostolic church at
Constantinople in 330.

What was the response of the church to this sudden
official acceptance? The sources that have come down
to us indicate an almost ecstatic enthusiasm for
Constantine. The emperor, the former chief opponent
of Christianity, had become its chief benefactor. He
now rebuilt its churches, gave it special donations,
and freed the bishops from political duties and
onerous taxes. He even imposed special taxes on
dissident factions in the church, like the Donatists
in North Africa. There seemed to be nothing about
which the church could raise any objections.

Eusebius of Caesarea, the church historian,
presented a view of the emperor which may have been
representative of many Christians. He concluded his
Ecclesiastical History with an account of the conflict
between Constantine and Licinius. According to him,
Licinius was an evil, treacherous, ungrateful
persecutor of Christianity and a blasphemer of God.
Constantine, on the other hand was patient, gentle,
godly and generous beyond the call of duty in dealing
with Licinius. Finally, reluctantly, Constantine had
been forced to dispose of Licinius in a battle in
order that the church would be freed from persecution.
In the battle Constantine and Crisipus "drew up their
forces on all sides against the enemies of the Deity
and won an easy victory."[45] Eusebius concluded the
history of the church with the story of Constantine's
successful unification of the empire. It seemed that
for Eusebius, God had been leading the church up to
this glorious moment. Constantine was God's chosen

instrument for bringing about the victory of the
church.

In the <u>Life of Constantine</u>, Eusebius lauded
Constantine and compared his piety with the pagan
brutality of his rivals.[46] Among the benefits that
Constantine had bestowed upon the church was the
restoration of the rights of those soldiers who had
been deprived of their rank by Licinius.[47] Military
rank rather than rejection of military service was now
coveted.

There was no hint in Eusebius that he saw any
problem in Christians fighting in the imperial army.
Nor did he see any problem in requesting divine help
for Constantine's wars. He lauded Constantine for
giving all Christians in the imperial service,
including soldiers, Sunday as a day of rest in which
they could worship God. Pagan soldiers were ordered
to gather in a separate place on the Lord's Day and
recite prayers which they had learned from memory.[48]

Other prominent churchmen agreed with Eusebius'
view of Constantine. Diodor of Tarsus declared that
God had worked through the church and through the
empire to bring about peace.[49] Jerome saw in the "Pax
Romana" following Constantine the fulfillment of the
Old and New Testament promises of peace.

Constantine, his sons, and the latter fourth
century emperors granted Christianity more and more
privileges, so that under Theodosius II only
Christians were allowed to serve in the army. The
same requirement was demanded for holding civil
office. Faith in Jesus Christ, according to the
Nicene definition, became the test of loyalty to the
emperor.[50] Not only Christian faith, but theological
orthodoxy became a prerequisite for civil and military
participation.

During the long reign of Constantine some very
significant developments occurred which profoundly
affected the church's attitude to pacifism and war.
The relationship of church and world changed.
Tertullian and Origen saw the church and world as
being in opposition to each other. The church was
under the Lordship of God, and the world in its
various aspects such as immorality, idolatry, and
war-making was opposed to the Lord of the church.
Both communities were identifiable. The church was in
the world, but in a very real historical and
experiential sense, its priorities and practises were
not those of the world. In the third century a

gradual erosion of that distinction between church and
world even in regard to bearing the sword was
perceptible. Under Constantine and his successors the
distinction of church and world as separate historical
communities almost dissappeared. That which had been
the practise and life style of the world very largely
had become the practise and the life style of the
church. The church which had seen its mission as
bringing people to God had expanded that mission to
include supporting the state and ordering society.
The concept world was now revised to refer primarily
to non-Romans, or Persians or Germanic tribes. Or,
more significantly, the "world" was located in the
heart, in people's attitudes and inner desires.

The church redefined and expanded its mission. In
the second century, and again in the writings of
Tertullian and Origen, the mission of the church was
to bring people to salvation in Jesus Christ, and to
help them express their changed lordship in their
lives. The church was well aware that life in Christ
might result in suffering and maybe even martyrdom.
One accusation that the Church Fathers brought against
Gnostics was that they were willing to live so as to
avoid martyrdom even to the extent of offering incense
to the genius of the emperor. The church under
Constantine saw its mission also as bringing people to
salvation in Jesus Christ. But the Christians' new
life under the Lordship of Christ had to be expressed
not only in such a way that it expressed the gospel
and gave glory to God, it also included maintaining
the order and stability of the united Christian Roman
empire. Thus, differing theologies created disorder
and had to be resolved as quickly as possible in
councils. Pacifism, if practised by all the members
of the church, would leave the state defenseless and
thus pacifism would contribute to chaos and confusion.

For the church after Constantine, pacifism was not
a possible dimension of the lay person's expression of
Christian ethical life. The progression to that
conviction had been lengthy and gradual. And yet, the
church also remembered that in its past it had been
pacifist. It read the biblical admonitions to turn
the other cheek, to love the enemy, and to overcome
evil with good. After Constantine, only monks and
clergy were able to be exempt from military service.
The needs of the empire had dictated a significant
change in the life of the church. The question was
how the church would respond to that change

theologically.

IV. THE PACIFISM OF THE FEW BECOMES THE PACIFISM OF ALL

The church after Constantine was faced with the task of conceptualizing its new role in society and in the world. It had allowed itself to be adopted by the state. Christians were called upon to serve in the imperial army under the leadership of the church's most illustrious member, the emperor. The emperors, of course, fought their wars for the glory of God and the protection of the church.

Did this new situation mean that Christians should participate in all wars? Were all wars divinely sanctioned simply because they were being led by a Christian emperor? Eusebius' enthusiastic evaluation of the piety of Constantine's reign over against the brutality of his rivals suggested this. But under succeeding Christian emperors, the church realized that not all wars were just or justifiable, even if led by Christian emperors. Thus the need arose to discover some other standards for evaluating whether a war was just. Such standards would need to be over and above the emperor and be able to guide the church as to whether it could legitimately support an emperor in a war. One of the first to articulate some principles which would distinguish between just and unjust wars was Ambrose.

Ambrose (339-397) was a pretorian prefect of northern Italy when in 374 the Arian bishop died. The Christian population demanded that he become the bishop, and reluctantly he consented to this, going through the required baptism and ordination to the different offices in eight days.

Ambrose was one of the few early important Western theologians who was not situated in north Africa. He was much nearer to the seat of imperial authority than the North Africans were. In the West, after Constantine, the emperors tended to neglect Rome which was the stronghold of paganism, and took other cities as their captials. Theodosius I used Milan as his capital.

Ambrose also exemplified the western church's inclination to be slightly more suspicious of the designs and actions of emperors than the eastern church was. The western church felt that she was the pastor, counselor, and moral guide for all Christians,

including the emperor. Thus in A.D. 390, when Ambrose
heard that emperor Theodosius I had massacred 6000
Thessalonians in a fit of anger, Ambrose refused him
the eucharist and even a seat in the assembly.   He
demanded that first Theodosius repent and do penance.
That Theodosius did repent publicly is evidence of the
western bishop's growing authority, and of his
willingness to subject an emperor's actions to
critique.

Ambrose was faced with the history of Christian
participation in the army. He did not raise the
question as to whether it was proper for Christians to
serve in the army. rather, he turned his attention to
the question whether Christians ought to fight in any
and all wars which the Christian emperors might
undertake.   Did the fact that the emperor was
Christian legitimate every war which was fought under
his authority?

Ambrose was too suspicious of emperors and their
susceptibility to base motivations to agree to this.
He probably developed this view during his service as
a pretorian prefect. Fully cognizant of the Roman
legal tradition, he argued that there existed a number
of criteria which were independent of an emperor and
according to which the wars or proposed wars could be
judged and evaluated.   Ambrose said that those wars
which were "legitimate" according to certain natural
and universal laws were wars in which Christians could
fight without denying God or contravening his
intentions for humanity.

In his treatise, Duties of the Clergy, Ambrose
discussed the basis of justice.[51] He was writing to
pagan philosophers and attempted to interpret
Christianity to them.   In this context he developed
principles which he said distinguished between just
and unjust wars. He began with the universally
accepted axiom that what chiefly characterizes a human
is reason.   From this premise of rationality, he
argued step by step that reason inevitably would lead
a person to piety, which is belief in God.

He also showed that a person's ethical life ought
to conform to the laws of reason, which is prudence.
Certainly if a person's reason could lead to piety,
then reason could also lead a person to an ethical
life acceptable to God.   Thus he said, it could be
shown on the basis of reason, what the criteria for a
just war are. He said that the piety of justice is
"first directed towards God, secondly towards one's

country, next towards parents, and lastly towards all.
This too, is in accordance with the guidance of
nature."[52]

On the basis of piety, the Christian's concern
ought to be first for others, not for self. To be
concerned for self and for the person's own safety
would be selfish and certainly piety toward God
required a person to be unselfish.

On the basis of reason it was clear that a
person's first concern ought to be for those nearest
to the person. Thus he said it was eminently just to
go to war against barbarians on behalf of one's
country and family, and to defend it and one's
neighbor against robbers.

Ambrose did not explain why it was rationally more
just to love one's neighbor, family or country than a
foreigner, barbarian or enemy. It is clear, though,
that this line of reasoning did not originate with
him, for in the whole section on the just war he
referred to Cicero's On Duties, in which Cicero[53]
developed the Roman empire's criteria of a just war.
Cicero's criteria are very similar to the ones Ambrose
mentioned. First, the assumption is that justice is
on "our" side. Second, since "our" cause is just,
this is sufficient justification to participate in the
war. Third, the excuse for going to war is that we
may live in peace unharmed. Fourth, Cicero outlined
various restrictions on the actual prosecution of a
war. For example, those who were conquered ought to
be shown consideration.[54]

Ambrose also spoke to the question of the use of
the sword. Consistent with his discussion on the just
war, he said that for the Christian not to take up the
sword in defence of his neighbor, family, and country
was to be selfish. Those who had unselfish love in
their heart would be willing to take the sword and
even give up their life for their country. He implied
that rejection of the sword was an expression of
selfish love and was essentially a position based on
lack of faith in God.

Ambrose, however, conceded that clerics and monks
ought not to take up the sword even in defense of the
country of family, for they had a different vocation.
Those who fight in wars, he said, fight for the
present, and so use means which are necessary and
appropriate for the present. The priest and monk,
however, fight for the future, and should use means
appropriate for the future kingdom.

Augustine (354-430), the bishop of Hippo, was the last great North African churchman. He was born a pagan. In his search for truth he moved from Manichaeism to neo-Platonism to Christianity, and it was in neo-Platonism that he discovered what were for him some key concepts.[55] In contrast to Manichaeism's materialism, he discovered that Being is spiritual. In contrast to a God who was conceived as material, he now discovered a God who was pure spirit and the source of all that is spiritual. He learned that the greatest good, the summum bonum for which people search, is God. Those who disbelieve in God search for lesser, baser, material things. They search for things, not the source of all Being.

On the question of war and peace, Augustine did not write any one extensive treatise on the subject. One has to sift through his writings for references to the issue. From these a rather coherent position emerges. In his discussion about peace and war, he was influenced by the conflict with Donatism in North Africa in which he at first counseled patience and dialogue but finally encouraged the use of the sword.[56] He also witnessed the fall of the eternal city, Rome, before the Germanic armies in 410. Toward the end of his life, North Africa was fighting for its life before Vandal armies. Augustine died in 430, the year that Hippo fell to the Vandals.

Augustine lived in a Christian Roman empire which was facing collapse due to dissension within and attacks from without. The situation was particularly serious in the western half of the empire. The defence of the gradually merging church and empire was a very immediate issue for Augustine. In this context, Augustine accepted the growing tradition that clerics should be pacifist. He, like Ambrose, also made a distinction between clerics who minister for the kingdom that is above, and lay Christians who live in the kingdom that is below. In addition to the vocational distinction, he also distinguished between those who lived more "God directed" lives, and those who were still more directed toward lower things.

Augustine also accepted Ambrose's criteria for a just war.[57] These can be categorized into six main criteria. First, the war must be just as to its intent—which is to restore peace. Peace for him, was the concord exhibited in the harmony of the universe. Second, the object of war must be to vindicate justice. His concept of justice was vague, although, he said, those wars are defined as just which avenge injuries.   Third,   the   war   must   be   just   as   to disposition,   which is Christian love.   Love is not incompatible   with   killing   because   love   and nonresistance are inward dispositions.   Fourth, the war must be just as to its auspices.   It is to be waged only under the authority of a legitimate ruler. This excluded revolutions.   Fifth, the conduct of war must be just.   Faith must be kept with the enemy. There should be no wanton violence, profanation of temples,   looting,   massacre,   or   conflagration. Vengeance, atrocities and reprisals were excluded, though ambush he allowed.   Sixth, only those in public authority could take life.   A private person would not be   able   to   defend   himself   without   passion, self-assertion, and a loss of love.

Augustine was, however, faced with the problem that Ambrose's criteria for a just war resulted in an ethic which did not take seriously the bibilical admonition to love the enemy, e.g. Matthew 5:44-48 and Romans 12:17-21.   Ambrose seemed to justify lesser love to the enemy and thereby justified taking up the sword against the enemy.   A second problem was that the vocational separation of Christians into clergy and laity meant that an important biblical injunction could only be expressed by a few.   Only the clergy could express the "agape" love which was basic to pacifism, and all other Christians were denied the possibility of expressing that love which loves even the enemy.

Augustine solved both these problems in a new interpretation of pacifism.   His answer came out of the heart of his theological concern.   Ontologically Augustine accepted a monistic view of reality.   All Being was on a continuum from pure Being, or God, to non-Being, even though he rejected the Neoplatonic view of emanation and emphasized creation.   That which was spiritual was closer to pure Being than that which was material.   The human person, who was composed of both soul and body, had had the possibility of directing his will toward that which was above, God, or toward things which were below.   In Adam the human will had been warped and humanity had lost the ability of God-directed "agape" love.[58]   But in Christ the human will had again been freed for the possibility of a God-directed life.

But, Augustine said, the God-directed life was not primarily a matter of outer action.   Rather, the issue was whether the inner, spiritual life was expressing love toward God. If the inner disposition was God-directed, then externals, such as acts of violence, could not disturb the inner attitude. It was an axiom of neo-Platonic ontology that lower, physical, material things could not affect that which was higher and spiritual.

Thus Augustine was provided with an ontology and anthropology within which he could take the New Testament pacifist teachings seriously and make them relevant for every Christian. In the Reply to Faustus the Manichaean he wrote:

"If it is supposed that God could not enjoin warfare because in after times it was said by the Lord Jesus Christ 'I say unto you that you resist not evil: but if any one strike thee on the right cheek, turn to him the left also,' the answer is that what is here required is not a bodily action, but an inward disposition."[59]

Every Christian should have love in his heart for both friend and enemy, contended Augustine. Love for the enemy should remain constant, even if the state or, as Augustine says, Christian duty should call upon the Christian to take up the sword to slay that enemy. The Christian would still continue to love the enemy, for he would kill out of duty and not out of malice. Only a non-Christian would kill an enemy out of malice. The Christian would continue to love his enemy and accept that in God's infinite wisdom it had become his lot to discipline the person, even if it meant taking his life. It would be his duty to obey that call.[60] As a parent restrains and punishes his child, so a Christian may be called upon to punish and restrain evil.

In regard to a pacifism which rejected the use of the sword for all Christians, Augustine had a ready reply. He said that such pacifism confused that which was higher and inner with that which was lower and outer. To demand that the outer person ought to express pacifist love to the enemy was to misunderstand the intention of the gospel message. Those who demanded the kind of pacifism which required all Christians to lay down the sword indicated by this that they had turned away from that which was higher, spiritual and God-directed, and were more concerned about things that were beneath. External pacifism could only arise in a context of unbelief.[61]

Augustine's theology of pacifism was profound and creative. Its influence in history is evidence of that. He brought order into the chaotic practise and theology of the church regarding war and peace. He was able to build on tradition; the long heritage of pacifism could be accepted and expressed by the clergy. He was able to provide an ethic that contributed toward order and stability in the empire. His creativity was most profound in that he was able to reinterpret pacifism so that it was not only expressible by the few clergy, but it could again become a necessary and possible way of life for all those who were in Christ. The pacifism of the few had again become the pacifism which all Christians could express.

The question, though, is whether Augustine's theology helped to elucidate the biblical teaching regarding peace, or whether it confused and distorted it. Another way to pose the question is to ask whether a different theology, based on assumptions other than the Neo-Platonic assumptions of Augustine, would not result in a fundamental reformulation of Augustine's understanding of peace and the role of war.

1. The patristic age generally includes the history of the early church up to the council of Chalcedon in 451.
2. The terms "pacifist" and "pacifism" will be used in this study. These terms are based on the Latin verb "pacificare" which consists of the two words pax (peace) and facere (to make). Pacifism thus expresses well the Biblical view that peace is an active process.
3. Hans Jonas, The Gnostic Religion (Boston: Beacon Press, 2nd ed. 1963); Elaine Pagels, The Gnostic Gospels (New York: The Random House, 1979); James M. Robinson, General Editor, The Nag Hammadi Library in English (New York: Harper & Row, Publishers, 1977).
4. Irenaeus, Against Haereses. See especially Book III.
5. Origen's principle theological treatise was Peri Archon.
6. The Contra Celsum is only extant in a Latin translation. Johannes Quasten, Patrology, Volume II (Utrecht - Antwerp: Spectrum Publishers, 1964), 52. Ante-Nicene Fathers, Volume IV, 395-669.
7. Contra Celsum, Book VIII, Chapter LV.
8. Contra Celsum, Book VIII, Chapter LVII.
9. Contra Celsum, Book VIII, Chapter LXXIV.
10. Contra Celsum, Book VIII, Chapter LXIX.
11. Contra Celsum, Book VIII, Chapter LXXII.
12. Contra Celsum, Book VIII, Chapter LXXIII.
13. Contra Celsum, Book VIII, Chapter LXXIII.
14. Contra Celsum, Book VIII, Chapter LXXIV.
15. Johannes Quasten, Patrology, Volume II 37-101.
16. ANF, Vol. III, 93-104.
17. De Corona Militis, Chapter I.
18. De Corona Militis, Chapter IV.
19. De Corona Militis, Chapter V.
20. De Corona Militis, Chapters VII and X.
21. De Corona Militis, Chapter XI.
22. De Corona Militis, Chapter XI.
23. De Corona Militis, Chapter XI.
24. De Corona Militis, Chapter XV.
25. De Corona Militis, Chapter XII.
26. De Corona Militis, Chapter XI.
27. Roland H. Bainton, Christian Attitudes to War and Peace (New York: Abingdon Press, 1960), 67f.

28. Lactantius, Divinae Institutiones, IV, XX
15-16; ANF, VII, 9-223; Arnobius, Adversus Nationes I,
6. ANF, VI, 413-540.
29. Eusebius, Historia Ecclesia, V, 5, 4-6, Nicene
and Post Nicene Fathers, Second Series, Vol. I, 386-7.
30. Bainton, War and Peace, 70.
31. Eusebius, Historia Ecclesia, VIII, 30, 8.
32. Bainton, War and Peace, 70.
33. Epistolae, XXXIII, 3, ANF, Volume 5, 312-314.
34. Eusebius, Historia Ecclesia, VIII, 1, 8.
35. Edward A. Ryan, "The Rejection of Military
Service by Early Christians," Theological Studies,
XIII, (1952), pp. 1-32; Leclerq, "Militarisme," in
Dictionnaire d'Archeologie Chretienne II (1933), pp.
1107-81, Gf, I, 294-97.
36. Matthew 5:9-11, 21-26, 38-48. J. B. Lightfoot,
The Apostolic Fathers "The Shepherd of Hermas" (Grand
Rapids: Baker Book House, 1976), 159-243.
37. Clement, Quis dives salvetur, ANF, II, 591-604.
38. Hippolytus, The Refutation of all Heresies, IX,
7, ANF, V, 128-131.
39. A Treatise Against the Heretic Novation, 6,
ANF, V, 657-656.
40. A Treatise Against the Heretic Novation, 7-9,
ANF, V, 659-660.
41. Arthur Vooebus, Einiges ueber die katitative
Taetigkeit des Syrischen Moenchtums, Ein Betrag zur
Geschichte der Liebestaetigkeit im Orient (Pinneberg,
1947); Celibacy, a Requirement for Baptism in the
Early Church (Louvain: Secretariat du Corpus SCO,
1965).
42. Regarding monasticism see: Hans Freiherr von
Campenhausen, Die Idee des Martyrium in der alten
Kirche (Goettingen: Vandenhoeck u. Ruprecht, 1964).
43. Arthur E. R. Boak, William G. Sinnigen, A
History of Rome to A.D. 565, 5th Edition (London:
Collier-MacMillan Limited, 1965), 430f.
44. For a recent analysis of Constantine's
acceptance of Christianity, see Alistair Kee,
Constantine versus Christ (London: SCM Press Ltd.,
1982).
45. Eusebius, Historia Ecclesia, X, 9, 1-9.
46. Eusebius, Vita Constantini, NPNF, Second
Series, Volume I, pp. 481-559.
47. Eusebius, Vita Constantini, Book. II, 33.
48. Eusebius, Vita Constantini, Book. IV, 18, 19.
49. Karl Staab, "Pauluskommentare aus der
griechischen Kirche," Neutestamentliche Abhandlungen,

XV, (1933), 107.

50. Clyde Pharr, editor, The Theodosian Code (Princeton: The Princeton University Press, 1952) p. 452f, states that the law of 395 A.D. ordered that no heretic could hold office in the imperial service. Furthermore, all heretics were to be deported from the imperial city.

51. Ambrose, Duties of the Clergy, NPNF, Series II, X, 22-25.

52. Ambrose, Duties of the Clergy, XXVII.

53. Cicero, De officiis. The Loeb Classical Library, Latin Series, Volume XXI, 3-424.

54. Ambrose, Duties of the Clergy, Books I, XXVII.

55. For a general survey of Augustine's life and works see: Berthold Altaner, Patrology, translated by Hilda C. Graff (New York: Herder and Herder, 1961), 487-534.

56. Augustine, Epistle 93, NPNF Series I Vol. I, 383.

57. Bainton, War and Peace, 95-98. The Augustinian writings on which these six criteria are based are: Epist. 189, 4-6; Epist. 47, 5; Epist. 138, ii, 14, 15; De Civitate Dei, XIX, 12-13; De Civitate Dei XXII, 6; De Civitate Dei I, 6-7; Quaest. Hept. VI, 10; Quaest. Hept. IV, 44; Contra Faustum XXII, 70, 75, 76, 79; Sermo Dom I, XX, 63, 70; En. Ps. CXXIV, 7.

58. De Civitate Dei, XIV, NPNF, Series I, Volume II, 1-511.

59. Contra Faustum, XXII, 76, NPNF, Series I, Volume IV, 155-345.

60. Contra Faustum, XXII, 74, 75; Sermo Dom, I, XX, 63.

61. Contra Faustum, XXII, 79; Epist 138, ii, 13-15.